career ideas for teens

in health science

Diane Lindsey Reeves
with **Gail Karlitz** and **Anna Prokos**

Checkmark Books
An imprint of Infobase Publishing

Career Ideas for Teens in Health Science

Copyright © 2006 by Bright Futures Press

All rights reserved. No part of this book may be reproduced or utilized in any form or by any means, electronic or mechanical, including photocopying, recording, or by any information storage or retrieval systems, without permission in writing from the publisher. For information contact:

Checkmark Books
An imprint of Infobase Publishing
132 West 31st Street
New York NY 10001

The Library of Congress has cataloged the hardcover edition as follows:

Reeves, Diane Lindsey, 1959–
    Career ideas for teens in health science / Diane Lindsey Reeves with Gail Karlitz and Anna Prokos.
        p. cm.
    Includes index.
    ISBN 0-8160-5290-5 (hc : alk. paper)
    1. Medicine—Vocational guidance. 2. Medical sciences—Vocational guidance. 3. Allied health personnel—Vocational guidance.   I. Karlitz, Gail. II. Prokos, Anna. III. Title.
    R690.R44 2004
    610.69—dc22

                                                                                    2004015040

ISBN: 0-8160-6920-4
Ferguson books are available at special discounts when purchased in bulk quantities for businesses, associations, institutions, or sales promotions. Please call our Special Sales Department in New York at (212) 967-8800 or (800) 322-8755.

You can find Ferguson on the World Wide Web at http://www.fergpubco.com

Text design by Joel and Sandy Armstrong
Cover design by Nora Wertz
Illustrations by Matt Wood

Printed in the United States of America

VB PKG 10 9 8 7 6 5 4 3 2 1

This book is printed on acid-free paper.

contents

acknowledgments

A million thanks to the people who took the time to share their career
stories and provide photos for this book:

Dr. Peter Anderson
Jan Braverman
Dr. John Cho
Dr. Marc Cutler
Dr. Tammi Davis
Dr. Brett Finkelstein
Patricia Kennedy
Aly Khan
Alexander Minevich
Anthony Mirabel
Dr. Michael Peters

And a big thank-you to our project interns and research assistants:

Susannah Driver
Lindsey Reeves

career ideas for teens

welcome to your future

Q: What's one of the most boring questions adults ask teens?

A: "So . . . what do you want to be when you grow up?"

Well-meaning adults always seem so interested in what you plan to be.

You, on the other hand, are just trying to make it through high school in one piece.

But you may still have a nagging feeling that you really need to find some direction and think about what you want to do with your life.

When it comes to choosing your life's work there's some good news and some bad news. The good news is that, according to the U.S. Bureau of Labor Statistics, you have more than 12,000 different occupations to choose from. With that many options there's got to be something that's just right for you.

Right?

Absolutely.

But . . .

Here comes the bad news.

THERE ARE MORE THAN 12,000 DIFFERENT OCCUPATIONS TO CHOOSE FROM!

How in the world are you ever going to figure out which one is right for you?

We're so glad you asked!

Helping high school students like you make informed choices about their future is what this book (and each of the other titles in the *Career Ideas for Teens* series) is all about. Here you'll encounter 10 tough questions designed to help you answer the biggest one of all: "What in the world am I going to do after I graduate from high school?"

The *Career Ideas for Teens* series enables you to expand your horizons beyond the "doctor, teacher, lawyer" responses common to those new to the career exploration process. The books provide a no-pressure introduction to real jobs that real people do. And they offer a chance to "try on" different career options before committing to a specific college program or career path. Each title in this series is based on one of the 16 career clusters established by the U.S. Department of Education.

And what is a career cluster, you ask? Career clusters are based on a simple and very useful concept. Each cluster consists of all entry-level through professional-level occupations in a broad industry area. All of the jobs and industries in a cluster have many things in common. This organizational structure makes it easier for people like you to get a handle on the big world of work. So instead of rushing headlong into a mind-boggling exploration of the entire universe of career opportunities, you get a chance to tiptoe into smaller, more manageable segments first.

We've used this career cluster concept to organize the *Career Ideas for Teens* series of books. For example, careers related to the arts, communication, and entertainment are organized or "clustered" into the *Career Ideas for Teens in the Arts and Communications* title; a wide variety of health care professions are included in *Career Ideas for Teens in Health Science*; and so on.

Clueless as to what some of these industries are all about? Can't even imagine how something like manufacturing or public administration could possibly relate to you?

No problem.

You're about to find out. Just be prepared to expect the unexpected as you venture out into the world of work. There are some pretty incredible options out there, and some pretty surprising ones too. In fact, it's quite possible that you'll discover that the ideal career for you is one you had never heard of before.

Whatever you do, don't cut yourself short by limiting yourself to just one book in the series. You may find that your initial interests guide you towards the health sciences field—which would, of course, be a good place to start. However, you may discover some new "twists" with a look through the arts and communications book. There you may find a way to blend your medical interests with your exceptional writing and speaking skills by considering becoming a public relations (PR) specialist for a hospital or pharmaceutical company. Or look at the book on education to see about becoming a public health educator or school nurse.

Before you get started, you should know that this book is divided into three sections, each representing an important step toward figuring out what to do with your life.

The first titles in the *Career Ideas for Teens* series focus on:

- Arts and Communications
- Education and Training
- Health Science
- Information Technology
- Law and Public Safety

Before You Get Started

Unlike most books, this one is meant to be actively experienced, rather than merely read. Passive perusal won't cut it. Energetic engagement is what it takes to figure out something as important as the rest of your life.

As we've already mentioned, you'll encounter 10 important questions as you work your way through this book. Following each Big Question is an activity designated with a symbol that looks like this:

Every time you see this symbol, you'll know it's time to invest a little energy in your future by getting out your notebook or binder, a pen or pencil, and doing whatever the instructions direct you to do. If this book is your personal property, you can choose to do the activities right in the book. But you still might want to make copies of your finished products to go in a binder so they are all in one place for easy reference.

When you've completed all the activities, you'll have your own personal **Big Question AnswerBook**, a planning guide representing a straightforward and truly effective process you can use throughout your life to make fully informed career decisions.

discover you at work

This first section focuses on a very important subject: You. It poses four Big Questions that are designed specifically to help you "discover you":

? Big Question #1: **who are you?**
? Big Question #2: **what are your interests and strengths?**
? Big Question #3: **what are your work values?**

Then, using an interest assessment tool developed by the U.S. Department of Labor and implemented with your very vivid imagination, you'll picture yourself doing some of the things that people actually do for their jobs. In other words, you'll start "discovering you at work" by answering the following:

? Big Question #4: **what's your work personality?**

Unfortunately, this first step is often a misstep for many people. Or make that a "missed" step. When you talk with the adults in your life about their career choices, you're likely to find that some of them never even considered the idea of choosing a career based on personal preferences and strengths. You're also likely to learn that if they had it to do over again, this step would definitely play a significant role in the choices they would make.

explore your options

There's more than meets the eye when it comes to finding the best career to pursue. There are also countless ways to blend talent or passion in these areas in some rather unexpected and exciting ways. Get ready to find answers to two more Big Questions as you browse through an entire section of career profiles:

❓ Big Question #5: **do you have the right skills?**
❓ Big Question #6: **are you on the right path?**

experiment with success

At long last you're ready to give this thing called career planning a trial run. Here's where you'll encounter three Big Questions that will unleash critical decision-making strategies and skills that will serve you well throughout a lifetime of career success.

While you're at it, take some time to sit in on a roundtable discussion with successful professionals representing a very impressive array of careers related to this industry. Many of their experiences will apply to your own life, even if you don't plan to pursue the same careers.

❓ Big Question #7: **who knows what you need to know?**
❓ Big Question #8: **how can you find out what a career is really like?**
❓ Big Question #9: **how do you know when you've made the right choice?**

Then as you begin to pull all your new insights and ideas together, you'll come to one final question:

❓ Big Question #10: **what's next?**

As you get ready to take the plunge, remember that this is a book about possibilities and potential. You can use it to make the most of your future work!

Here's what you'll need to complete the Big Question AnswerBook:

- A notebook or binder for the completed activities included in all three sections of the book
- An openness to new ideas
- Complete and completely candid answers to the 10 Big Question activities

So don't just read it, do it.
Plan it.
Dream it.

SECTION 1

discover you at work

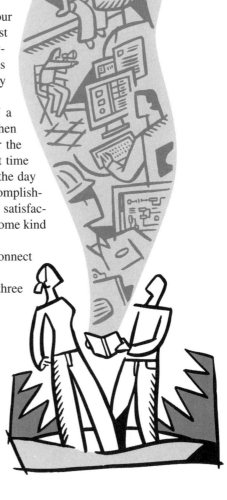

The goal here is to get some clues about who you are and what you should do with your life. As time goes by, you will grow older, become more educated, and have more experiences, but many things that truly define you are not likely to change. Even now you possess very strong characteristics —genuine qualities that mark you as the unique and gifted person that you undoubtedly are.

It's impossible to overestimate the importance of giving your wholehearted attention to this step. You, after all, are the most valuable commodity you'll ever have to offer a future employer. Finding work that makes the most of your assets often means the difference between enjoying a rewarding career and simply earning a paycheck.

You've probably already experienced the satisfaction of a good day's work. You know what we mean—those days when you get all your assignments in on time, you're prepared for the pop quiz your teacher sprung on you, and you beat your best time during sports practice. You may be exhausted at the end of the day but you can't help but feel good about yourself and your accomplishments. A well-chosen career can provide that same sense of satisfaction. Since you're likely to spend upwards of 40 years doing some kind of work, well-informed choices make a lot of sense!

Let's take a little time for you to understand yourself and connect what you discover about yourself to the world of work.

To find a career path that's right for you, we'll tackle these three Big Questions first:

- **who are you?**
- **what are your interests and strengths?**
- **what are your work values?**

Big Question #1:
who are you?

Have you ever noticed how quickly new students in your school or new families in your community find the people who are most like them? If you've ever been the "new" person yourself, you've probably spent your first few days sizing up the general population and then getting in with the people who dress in clothes a lot like yours, appreciate the same style of music, or maybe even root for the same sports teams.

Given that this process happens so naturally—if not necessarily on purpose—it should come as no surprise that many people lean toward jobs that surround them with people most like them. When people with common interests, common values, and complementary talents come together in the workplace, the results can be quite remarkable.

Many career aptitude tests, including the one developed by the U.S. Department of Labor and included later in this book, are based on the theory that certain types of people do better at certain types of jobs. It's like a really sophisticated matchmaking service. Take your basic strengths and interests and match them to the strengths and interests required by specific occupations.

It makes sense when you think about it. When you want to find a career that's ideally suited for you, find out what people like you are doing and head off in that direction!

There's just one little catch.

The only way to recognize other people like you is to recognize yourself. Who are you anyway? What are you like? What's your basic approach to life and work?

Now's as good a time as any to find out. Let's start by looking at who you are in a systematic way. This process will ultimately help you understand how to identify personally appropriate career options.

 Big Activity #1:
who are you?

On a sheet of paper, if this book doesn't belong to you, create a list of adjectives that best describe you. You should be able to come up with at least 15 qualities that apply to you. There's no need to make judgments about whether these qualities are good or bad. They just are. They represent who you are and can help you understand what you bring to the workforce.

(If you get stuck, ask a trusted friend or adult to help describe especially strong traits they see in you.)

Some of the types of qualities you may choose to include are:

- **How you relate to others:**
  Are you shy? Outgoing? Helpful? Dependent? Empathic? In charge? Agreeable? Challenging? Persuasive? Popular? Impatient? A loner?
- **How you approach new situations:**
  Are you adventurous? Traditional? Cautious? Enthusiastic? Curious?
- **How you feel about change—planned or unplanned:**
  Are you resistant? Adaptable? Flexible? Predictable?
- **How you approach problems:**
  Are you persistent? Spontaneous? Methodical? Creative?
- **How you make decisions:**
  Are you intuitive? Logical? Emotional? Practical? Systematic? Analytical?
- **How you approach life:**
  Are you laid back? Ambitious? Perfectionist? Idealistic? Optimistic? Pessimistic? Self-sufficient?

Feel free to use any of these words if they happen to describe you well, but please don't limit yourself to this list. Pick the best adjectives that paint an accurate picture of the real you. Get more ideas from a dictionary or thesaurus if you'd like.

When you're finished, put the completed list in your Big Question AnswerBook.

Big Activity #1: **who are you?**

fifteen qualities that describe me

1	2	3
4	5	6
7	8	9
10	11	12
13	14	15

etc.

Big Question #2:
what are your interests and strengths?

For many people, doing something they like to do is the most important part of deciding on a career path—even more important than how much money they can earn!

We don't all like to do the same things—and that's good. For some people, the ideal vacation is lying on a beach, doing absolutely nothing; others would love to spend weeks visiting museums and historic places. Some people wish they had time to learn to skydive or fly a plane; others like to learn to cook gourmet meals or do advanced math.

If we all liked the same things, the world just wouldn't work very well. There would be incredible crowds in some places and ghost towns in others. Some of our natural resources would be overburdened; others would never be used. We would all want to eat at the same restaurant, wear the same outfit, see the same movie, and live in the same place. How boring!

So let's get down to figuring out what you most like to do and how you can spend your working life doing just that. In some ways your answer to this question is all you really need to know about choosing a career, because the people who enjoy their work the most are those who do something they enjoy. We're not talking rocket science here. Just plain old common sense.

Big Activity # 2:
what are your interests and strengths?

Imagine this: No school, no job, no homework, no chores, no obligations at all. All the time in the world you want to do all the things you like most. You know what we're talking about—those things that completely grab your interest and keep you engrossed for hours without your getting bored. Those kinds of things you do really well—sometimes effortlessly, sometimes with extraordinary (and practiced) skill.

And, by the way, EVERYONE has plenty of both interests and strengths. Some are just more visible than others.

Step 1: Write the three things you most enjoy doing on a sheet of paper, if this book doesn't belong to you. Leave lots of space after each thing.

Step 2: Think about some of the deeper reasons why you enjoy each of these activities—the motivations beyond "it's fun." Do you enjoy shopping because it gives you a chance to be with your friends? Because it allows you to find new ways to express your individuality? Because you enjoy the challenge of finding bargains or things no one else has discovered? Or because it's fun to imagine the lifestyle you'll be able to lead when you're finally rich and famous? In the blank spaces, record the reasons why you enjoy each activity.

Step 3: Keep this list handy in your Big Question AnswerBook so that you can refer to it any time you have to make a vocational decision. Sure, you may have to update the list from time to time as your interests change. But one thing is certain. The kind of work you'll most enjoy will be linked in some way to the activities on that list. Count on it.

Maybe one of your favorite things to do is "play basketball." Does that mean the only way you'll ever be happy at work is to play professional basketball?

Maybe.

Maybe not.

Use your *why* responses to read between the lines. The *whys* can prove even more important than the *what*s. Perhaps what you like most about playing basketball is the challenge or the chance to be part of a team that shares a common goal. Maybe you really like pushing yourself to improve. Or it could be the rush associated with competition and the thrill of winning.

The more you uncover your own *whys*, the closer you'll be to discovering important clues about the kinds of work that are best for you.

Big Activity #2: **what are your interests and strengths?**

things you enjoy doing	why you enjoy doing them
1	• • •
2	• • •
3	• • •

Big Question #3:
what are your work values?

Chances are, you've never given a moment's thought to this next question. At least not in the context of career planning.

You already looked at who you are and what you enjoy and do well. The idea being, of course, to seek out career options that make the most of your innate qualities, preferences, and natural abilities.

As you start checking into various careers, you'll discover one more dimension associated with making personally appropriate career choices. You'll find that even though people may have the exact same job title, they may execute their jobs in dramatically different ways. For instance, everyone knows about teachers. They teach things to other people. Period.

But wait. If you line up 10 aspiring teachers in one room, you may be surprised to discover how vastly different their interpretations of the job may be. There are the obvious differences, of course. One may want to teach young children; one may want to teach adults. One will focus on teaching math, while another one focuses on teaching Spanish.

Look a little closer and you'll find even greater disparity in the choices they make. One may opt for the prestige (and paycheck) of working in an Ivy League college, while another is completely committed to teaching disadvantaged children in a remote area of the Appalachian Mountains. One may approach teaching simply as a way to make a living, while another devotes almost every waking hour to working with his or her students.

These subtle but significant differences reflect what's truly important to each person. In a word, they reflect the person's values—those things that are most important to them.

People's values depend on many factors—their upbringing, their life experiences, their goals and ambitions, their religious beliefs, and, quite frankly, the way they view the world and their role in it. Very few people share exactly the same values. However, that doesn't necessarily mean that some people are right and others are wrong. It just means they have different perspectives.

Here's a story that shows how different values can be reflected in career choices.

Imagine: It's five years after college graduation and a group of college friends are back together for the first time. They catch up about their lives, their families, and their careers. Listen in on one of their reunion conversations and see if you can guess what each is doing now.

Alice: I have the best career. Every day I get the chance to help kids with special needs get a good education.

Bob: I love my career, too. It's great to know that I am making my town a safer place for everyone.

Cathy: It was tough for me to commit to more school after college. But I'm glad I did. After all I went through when my parents divorced, I'm glad I can be there to make things easier for other families.

David: I know how you feel. I'm glad I get to do something that helps companies function smoothly and keep our economy strong. Of course, you remember that I had a hard time deciding whether to pursue this career or teaching! This way I get the best of both worlds.

Elizabeth: It's great that we both ended up in the corporate world. You know that I was always intrigued by the stock market.

So exactly what is each of the five former freshman friends doing today? Have you made your guesses?

Alice is a lawyer. She specializes in education law. She makes sure that school districts provide special needs children with all of the resources they are entitled to under the law.

Bob is a lawyer. He is a prosecuting attorney and makes his town safer by ensuring that justice is served when someone commits a crime.

Cathy is a lawyer. She practices family law. She helps families negotiate separation and divorce agreements and makes sure that adoption and custody proceedings protect everyone involved. Sometimes she even provides legal intervention to protect adults or children who are in abusive situations.

David is a lawyer. He practices employment law. He helps companies set up policies that follow fair employment practices. He also gives seminars to managers, teaching them what the law says and means about sexual harassment, discrimination, and termination of employment.

Elizabeth is a lawyer. She practices corporate law and is indispensable to corporations with legal responsibilities towards stockholders and the government.

Wow! All five friends have the same job title. But each describes his/her job so differently! All five were able to enter the field of law and focus on the things that are most important to them: quality education, freedom from crime, protection of families and children, fairness in the workplace, and corporate economic growth. Identifying and honoring your personal values is an important part of choosing your life's work.

Big Activity #3:
what are your work values?

Step 1: Look at the following chart. If this book doesn't belong to you, divide a sheet of paper into the following three columns:
- **Essential**

Statements that fall into this column are very important to you. If the job doesn't satisfy these needs, you're not interested.
- **Okay**

Great if the job satisfies these needs, but you can also live without them.
- **No Way**

Statements that fall into this column represent needs that are not at all important to you or things you'd rather do without or simply couldn't tolerate.

Step 2: Look over the following list of statements representing different work values. Rewrite each statement in the appropriate column. Does the first statement represent something that is critical to you to have in your work? If so, write it in the first column. No big deal either way? Write it in the second column. Couldn't stand it? Write it in the third column. Repeat the same process for each of the value statements.

Step 3: When you're finished, place your complete work values chart in your Big Question AnswerBook.

Got it? Then get with it.

Really think about these issues. Lay it on the line. What values are so deeply ingrained in you that you'd be absolutely miserable if you had to sacrifice them for a job? Religious beliefs and political leanings fall into this category for some people.

Which ones provide room for some give and take? Things like vacation and benefits, working hours, and other issues along those lines may be completely negotiable for some people, but absolutely not for others.

Just remember, wherever you go and whatever you do, be sure that the choices you make are true to you.

Big Activity #3: **what are your work values?**

work values	essential	okay	no way
1. I can count on plenty of opportunity for advancement and taking on more responsibility.			
2. I can work to my fullest potential using all of my abilities.			
3. I would be able to give directions and instructions to others.			
4. I would always know exactly what my manager expects of me.			
5. I could structure my own day.			
6. I would be very busy all day.			
7. I would work in attractive and pleasant surroundings.			
8. My coworkers would be people I might choose as friends.			
9. I would get frequent feedback about my performance.			
10. I could continue my education to progress to an even higher level job.			
11. Most of the time I would be able to work alone.			
12. I would know precisely what I need to do to succeed at the job.			
13. I could make decisions on my own.			

Big Activity #3: **what are your work values?**

work values	essential	okay	no way
14. I would have more than the usual amount of vacation time.			
15. I would be working doing something I really believe in.			
16. I would feel like part of a team.			
17. I would find good job security and stable employment opportunities in the industry.			
18. I could depend on my manager for the training I need.			
19. I would earn lots of money.			
20. I would feel a sense of accomplishment in my work.			
21. I would be helping other people.			
22. I could try out my own ideas.			
23. I would not need to have further training or education to do this job.			
24. I would get to travel a lot.			
25. I could work the kind of hours I need to balance work, family, and personal responsibilities.			

To summarize in my own words, the work values most important to me include:

Big Question #4:
what is your work personality?

Congratulations. After completing the first three activities, you've already discovered a set of skills you can use throughout your life. Basing key career decisions on factors associated with who you are, what you enjoy and do well, and what's most important about work will help you today as you're just beginning to explore the possibilities, as well as into the future as you look for ways to cultivate your career.

Now that you've got that mastered, let's move on to another important skill. This one blends some of what you just learned about yourself with what you need to learn about the real world of work. It's a reality check of sorts as you align and merge your personal interests and abilities with those required in different work situations. At the end of this task you will identify your personal interest profile.

This activity is based on the work of Dr. John Holland. Dr. Holland conducted groundbreaking research that identified different characteristics in people. He found that he could classify people into six basic groups based on which characteristics tended to occur at the same time. He also found that the characteristics that defined the different groups of people were also characteristics that corresponded to success in different groups of occupations. The result of all that work was a classification system that identifies and names six distinct groups of people who share personal interests or characteristics and are likely to be successful in a group of clearly identified jobs.

Dr. Holland's work is respected by workforce professionals everywhere and is widely used by employers and employment agencies to help people get a handle on the best types of work to pursue.

The following Work Interest Profiler (WIP) is based on Dr. Holland's theories and was developed by the U.S. Department of Labor's Employment and Training Administration as part of an important project called O*Net. O*Net is a system used in all 50 states to provide career and employment services to thousands of people every year. It's a system you'll want to know about when it's time to take that first plunge into the world of work. If you'd like, you can find more information about this system at ***http://online.onetcenter.org***.

Big Activity #4:

what is your work personality?

By completing O*Net's Work Interest Profiler (WIP), you'll gain valuable insight into the types of work that are right for you.

here's how it works

The WIP lists many activities that real people do at real jobs. Your task is to read a brief statement about each of these activities and decide if it is something you think you'd enjoy doing. Piece of cake!

Don't worry about whether you have enough education or training to perform the activity. And, for now, forget about how much money you would make performing the activity.

Just boil it down to whether or not you'd like performing each work activity. If you'd like it, put a check in the *like* column that corresponds to each of the six interest areas featured in the test on the handy dandy chart you're about to create (or use the one in the book if it's yours). If you don't like it, put that check in the *dislike* column. What if you don't have a strong opinion on a particular activity? That's okay. Count that one as *unsure*.

Be completely honest with yourself. No one else is going to see your chart. If you check things you think you "should" check, you are not helping yourself find the career that will make you happy.

Before you start, create a chart for yourself. Your scoring sheet will have six horizontal rows and three vertical columns. Label the six rows as Sections 1 through 6, and label the three columns *like*, *dislike*, and *unsure*.

how to complete the Work Interest Profiler

Step 1: Start with Section 1.

Step 2: Look at the first activity and decide whether you would like to do it as part of your job.

Step 3: Put a mark in the appropriate column (*Like*, *Dislike*, or *Unsure*) on the Section 1 row.

Step 4: Continue for every activity in Section 1. Then do Sections 2 through 6.

Step 5: When you've finished all of the sections, count the number of marks you have in each column and write down the total.

Remember, this is not a test! There are no right or wrong answers. You are completing this profile to learn more about yourself and your work-related interests.

Also, once you've completed this activity, be sure to put your chart and any notes in your Big Question AnswerBook.

Ready? Let's go!

Section 1

1. Drive a taxi
2. Repair household appliances
3. Catch fish as a member of a fishing crew
4. Paint houses
5. Assemble products in a factory
6. Install flooring in houses
7. Perform lawn care services
8. Drive a truck to deliver packages to homes and offices
9. Work on an offshore oil-drilling rig
10. Put out forest fires
11. Fix a broken faucet
12. Refinish furniture
13. Guard money in an armored car
14. Lay brick or tile
15. Operate a dairy farm
16. Raise fish in a fish hatchery
17. Build a brick walkway
18. Enforce fish and game laws
19. Assemble electronic parts
20. Build kitchen cabinets
21. Maintain the grounds of a park
22. Operate a motorboat to carry passengers
23. Set up and operate machines to make products
24. Spray trees to prevent the spread of harmful insects
25. Monitor a machine on an assembly line

Section 2

1. Study space travel
2. Develop a new medicine
3. Study the history of past civilizations
4. Develop a way to better predict the weather
5. Determine the infection rate of a new disease
6. Study the personalities of world leaders
7. Investigate the cause of a fire
8. Develop psychological profiles of criminals
9. Study whales and other types of marine life
10. Examine blood samples using a microscope
11. Invent a replacement for sugar
12. Study genetics
13. Do research on plants or animals
14. Study weather conditions
15. Investigate crimes
16. Study ways to reduce water pollution
17. Develop a new medical treatment or procedure
18. Diagnose and treat sick animals
19. Conduct chemical experiments
20. Study rocks and minerals
21. Do laboratory tests to identify diseases
22. Study the structure of the human body
23. Plan a research study
24. Study the population growth of a city
25. Make a map of the bottom of the ocean

Section 3

1. Paint sets for a play
2. Create special effects for movies
3. Write reviews of books or movies
4. Compose or arrange music
5. Design artwork for magazines
6. Pose for a photographer
7. Create dance routines for a show
8. Play a musical instrument
9. Edit movies
10. Sing professionally
11. Announce a radio show
12. Perform stunts for a movie or television show
13. Design sets for plays
14. Act in a play
15. Write a song
16. Perform jazz or tap dance
17. Sing in a band
18. Direct a movie
19. Write scripts for movies or television shows
20. Audition singers and musicians for a musical show
21. Conduct a musical choir
22. Perform comedy routines in front of an audience
23. Dance in a Broadway show
24. Perform as an extra in movies, plays, or television shows
25. Write books or plays

Section 4

1. Teach children how to play sports
2. Help people with family-related problems
3. Teach an individual an exercise routine
4. Perform nursing duties in a hospital
5. Help people with personal or emotional problems
6. Teach work and living skills to people with disabilities
7. Assist doctors in treating patients
8. Work with juveniles on probation
9. Supervise the activities of children at a camp
10. Teach an elementary school class
11. Perform rehabilitation therapy
12. Help elderly people with their daily activities
13. Help people who have problems with drugs or alcohol
14. Teach a high school class
15. Give career guidance to people
16. Do volunteer work at a non-profit organization
17. Help families care for ill relatives
18. Teach sign language to people with hearing disabilities
19. Help people with disabilities improve their daily living skills
20. Help conduct a group therapy session
21. Work with children with mental disabilities
22. Give CPR to someone who has stopped breathing
23. Provide massage therapy to people
24. Plan exercises for patients with disabilities
25. Counsel people who have a life-threatening illness

Section 5

1. Sell CDs and tapes at a music store
2. Manage a clothing store
3. Sell houses
4. Sell computer equipment in a store
5. Operate a beauty salon or barber shop
6. Sell automobiles
7. Represent a client in a lawsuit
8. Negotiate business contracts
9. Sell a soft drink product line to stores and restaurants
10. Start your own business
11. Be responsible for the operations of a company
12. Give a presentation about a product you are selling
13. Buy and sell land
14. Sell restaurant franchises to individuals
15. Manage the operations of a hotel
16. Negotiate contracts for professional athletes
17. Sell merchandise at a department store
18. Market a new line of clothing
19. Buy and sell stocks and bonds
20. Sell merchandise over the telephone
21. Run a toy store
22. Sell hair-care products to stores and salons
23. Sell refreshments at a movie theater
24. Manage a retail store
25. Sell telephone and other communication equipment

Section 6

1. Develop an office filing system
2. Generate the monthly payroll checks for an office
3. Proofread records or forms
4. Schedule business conferences
5. Enter information into a database
6. Photocopy letters and reports
7. Keep inventory records
8. Record information from customers applying for charge accounts
9. Load computer software into a large computer network
10. Use a computer program to generate customer bills
11. Develop a spreadsheet using computer software
12. Operate a calculator
13. Direct or transfer office phone calls
14. Use a word processor to edit and format documents
15. Transfer funds between banks, using a computer
16. Compute and record statistical and other numerical data
17. Stamp, sort, and distribute office mail
18. Maintain employee records
19. Record rent payments
20. Keep shipping and receiving records
21. Keep accounts payable/receivable for an office
22. Type labels for envelopes and packages
23. Calculate the wages of employees
24. Take notes during a meeting
25. Keep financial records

Section 1
Realistic

	Like	Dislike	Unsure
1.			
2.			
3.			
4.			
5.			
6.			
7.			
8.			
9.			
10.			
11.			
12.			
13.			
14.			
15.			
16.			
17.			
18.			
19.			
20.			
21.			
22.			
23.			
24.			
25.			

Total Realistic

Section 2
Investigative

	Like	Dislike	Unsure
1.			
2.			
3.			
4.			
5.			
6.			
7.			
8.			
9.			
10.			
11.			
12.			
13.			
14.			
15.			
16.			
17.			
18.			
19.			
20.			
21.			
22.			
23.			
24.			
25.			

Total Investigative

Section 3
Artistic

	Like	Dislike	Unsure
1.			
2.			
3.			
4.			
5.			
6.			
7.			
8.			
9.			
10.			
11.			
12.			
13.			
14.			
15.			
16.			
17.			
18.			
19.			
20.			
21.			
22.			
23.			
24.			
25.			

Total Artistic

Section 4
Social

	Like	Dislike	Unsure
1.			
2.			
3.			
4.			
5.			
6.			
7.			
8.			
9.			
10.			
11.			
12.			
13.			
14.			
15.			
16.			
17.			
18.			
19.			
20.			
21.			
22.			
23.			
24.			
25.			

Total Social

Section 5
Enterprising

	Like	Dislike	Unsure
1.			
2.			
3.			
4.			
5.			
6.			
7.			
8.			
9.			
10.			
11.			
12.			
13.			
14.			
15.			
16.			
17.			
18.			
19.			
20.			
21.			
22.			
23.			
24.			
25.			

Total Enterprising

Section 6
Conventional

	Like	Dislike	Unsure
1.			
2.			
3.			
4.			
5.			
6.			
7.			
8.			
9.			
10.			
11.			
12.			
13.			
14.			
15.			
16.			
17.			
18.			
19.			
20.			
21.			
22.			
23.			
24.			
25.			

Total Conventional

What are your top three work personalities? List them here if this is your own book or on a separate piece of paper if it's not.

1. _____
2. _____
3. _____

all done? let's see what it means

Be sure you count up the number of marks in each column on your scoring sheet and write down the total for each column. You will probably notice that you have a lot of *likes* for some sections, and a lot of *dislikes* for other sections. The section that has the most *likes* is your primary interest area. The section with the next highest number of *likes* is your second interest area. The next highest is your third interest area.

Now that you know your top three interest areas, what does it mean about your work personality type? We'll get to that in a minute, but first we are going to answer a couple of other questions that might have crossed your mind:

- What is the best work personality to have?
- What does my work personality mean?

First of all, there is no "best" personality in general. There is, however, a "best" personality for each of us. It's who we really are and how we feel most comfortable. There may be several "best" work personalities for any job because different people may approach the job in different ways. But there is no "best work personality."

Asking about the "best work personality" is like asking whether the "best" vehicle is a sports car, a sedan, a station wagon, or a sports utility vehicle. It all depends on who you are and what you need.

One thing we do know is that our society needs all of the work personalities in order to function effectively. Fortunately, we usually seem to have a good mix of each type.

So, while many people may find science totally boring, there are many other people who find it fun and exciting. Those are the people who invent new technologies, who become doctors and researchers, and who turn natural resources into the things we use every day. Many people may think that spending a day with young children is unbearable, but those who love that environment are the teachers, community leaders, and museum workers that nurture children's minds and personalities.

When everything is in balance, there's a job for every person and a person for every job.

Now we'll get to your work personality. Following are descriptions of each of Dr. Holland's six work personalities that correspond to the six sections in your last exercise. You, like most people, are a unique combination of more than one. A little of this, a lot of that. That's what makes us interesting.

Identify your top three work personalities. Also, pull out your responses to the first three exercises we did. As you read about your top three work personalities, see how they are similar to the way you described yourself earlier.

Type 1
Realistic

Realistic people are often seen as the "Doers." They have mechanical or athletic ability and enjoy working outdoors.

Realistic people like work activities that include practical, hands-on problems and solutions. They enjoy dealing with plants, animals, and real-life materials like wood, tools, and machinery.

Careers that involve a lot of paperwork or working closely with others are usually not attractive to realistic people.

Who you are:
independent
reserved
practical
mechanical
athletic
persistent

What you like to do/what you do well:
build things
train animals
play a sport
fix things
garden
hunt or fish
woodworking

repair cars
refinish furniture

Career possibilities:
aerospace engineer
aircraft pilot
animal breeder
architect
baker/chef
building inspector
carpenter
chemical engineer
civil engineer
construction manager
dental assistant
detective
glazier
jeweler
machinist
oceanographer
optician
park ranger
plumber
police officer
practical nurse
private investigator
radiologist
sculptor

Type 2
Investigative

Investigative people are often seen as the "Thinkers." They much prefer searching for facts and figuring out problems mentally to doing physical activity or leading other people.

If Investigative is one of your strong interest areas, your answers to the earlier exercises probably matched some of these:

Who you are:
curious
logical
independent
analytical
observant
inquisitive

What you like to do/what you do well:
think abstractly
solve problems
use a microscope
do research
fly a plane
explore new subjects
study astronomy
do puzzles
work with a computer

Career possibilities:

aerospace engineer
archaeologist
CAD technician
chemist
chiropractor
computer programmer
coroner
dentist
electrician
ecologist
geneticist
hazardous waste technician
historian
horticulturist
management consultant
medical technologist
meteorologist
nurse practitioner
pediatrician
pharmacist
political scientist
psychologist
software engineer
surgeon
technical writer
veterinarian
zoologist

Type 3
Artistic

Artistic people are the "Creators." People with this primary interest like work activities that deal with the artistic side of things.

Artistic people need to have the opportunity for self-expression in their work. They want to be able to use their imaginations and prefer to work in less structured environments, without clear sets of rules about how things should be done.

Who you are:

imaginative
intuitive
expressive
emotional
creative
independent

What you like to do/what you do well:

draw
paint
play an instrument
visit museums
act
design clothes or rooms
read fiction
travel
write stories, poetry, or music

Career possibilities:

architect
actor
animator
art director
cartoonist
choreographer
costume designer
composer
copywriter
dancer
disc jockey
drama teacher
emcee
fashion designer
graphic designer
illustrator
interior designer
journalist
landscape architect
medical illustrator
photographer
producer
scriptwriter
set designer

Type 4
Social

Social people are known as the "Helpers." They are interested in work that can assist others and promote learning and personal development.

Communication with other people is very important to those in the Social group. They usually do not enjoy jobs that require a great amount of work with objects, machines, or data. Social people like to teach, give advice, help, cure, or otherwise be of service to people.

Who you are:
friendly
outgoing
empathic
persuasive
idealistic
generous

What you like to do/what you do well:
teach others
work in groups
play team sports
care for children
go to parties
help or advise others
meet new people
express yourself
join clubs or organizations

Career possibilities:
animal trainer
arbitrator
art teacher
art therapist
audiologist
child care worker
clergy person
coach
counselor/therapist
cruise director
dental hygienist
employment interviewer
EMT worker
fitness trainer
flight attendant
occupational therapist
police officer
recreational therapist
registered nurse
school psychologist
social worker
substance abuse counselor
teacher
tour guide

Type 5
Enterprising

Enterprising work personalities can be called the "Persuaders." These people like work activities that have to do with starting up and carrying out projects, especially business ventures. They like taking risks for profit, enjoy being responsible for making decisions, and generally prefer action to thought or analysis.

People in the Enterprising group like to work with other people. While the Social group focuses on helping other people, members of the Enterprising group are able to lead, manage, or persuade other people to accomplish the goals of the organization.

Who you are:
assertive
self-confident
ambitious
extroverted
optimistic
adventurous

What you like to do/what you do well:
organize activities
sell things
promote ideas

discuss politics
hold office in clubs
give talks or speeches
meet people
initiate projects
start your own business

Career possibilities:
advertising
chef
coach, scout
criminal investigator
economist
editor
foreign service officer
funeral director
hotel manager
journalist
lawyer
lobbyist
public relations specialist
newscaster
restaurant manager
sales manager
school principal
ship's captain
stockbroker
umpire, referee
urban planner

Type 6 Conventional

People in the Conventional group are the "Organizers." They like work activities that follow set procedures and routines. They are more comfortable and proficient working with data and detail than they are with generalized ideas.

Conventional people are happiest in work situations where the lines of authority are clear, where they know exactly what responsibilities are expected of them, and where there are precise standards for the work.

Who you are:
well-organized
accurate
practical
persistent
conscientious
ambitious

What you like to do/what you do well:
work with numbers
type accurately
collect or organize things
follow up on tasks
be punctual
be responsible for details
proofread

keep accurate records
understand regulations

Career possibilities:
accountant
actuary
air traffic controller
assessor
budget analyst
building inspector
chief financial officer
corporate treasurer
cost estimator
court reporter
economist
environmental compliance
lawyer
fire inspector
insurance underwriter
legal secretary
mathematician
medical secretary
proofreader
tax preparer

health science careers
work personality codes

Once you've discovered your own unique work personality code, you can use it to explore the careers profiled in this book and elsewhere. Do keep in mind though that this code is just a tool meant to help focus your search. It's not meant to box you in or to keep you from pursuing any career that happens to capture your imagination.

Following is a chart listing the work personality codes associated with each of the careers profiled in this book.

	Realistic	Investigative	Artistic	Social	Enterprising	Conventional
My Work Personality Code (mark your top three areas)						
Acupuncturist	X	X			X	
Art Therapist			X	X	X	
Athletic Trainer	X			X	X	
Audiologist	X	X			X	
Biochemist	X	X	X			
Bioinformatics Scientist	X	X			X	
Biomedical Engineer	X	X			X	
Chiropractor	X	X		X		
Computed Tomography Technologist	X	X			X	
Cytotechnologist	X	X				X
Dental Hygienist	X		X	X		
Dentist	X	X		X		
Dietician		X		X	X	
Electroneurodiagnostic Technologist		X	X	X		
Emergency Medical Technician	X	X			X	
Epidemiologist	X	X			X	

	Realistic	Investigative	Artistic	Social	Enterprising	Conventional
My Work Personality Code						
Forensic Pathologist		X	X		X	
Geneticist	X	X		X		
Home Health Aide	X			X	X	
Industrial Hygienist	X				X	X
Kinesiotherapist		X		X	X	
Massage Therapist	X			X	X	
Medical Technologist		X	X	X		
Microbiologist	X	X			X	
Mortician	X			X	X	
Nuclear Medicine Technician	X	X		X		
Nurse	X		X	X		
Occupational Therapist	X			X	X	
Optometrist	X	X				X
Pharmacist		X		X	X	
Phlebotomist	X	X		X		
Physical Therapist		X		X	X	
Physician		X		X		X
Physician Assistant		X	X	X		
Veterinarian	X	X		X		

Now it's time to move on to the next big step in the Big Question process. While the first step focused on you, the next one focuses on the world of work. It includes profiles of a wide variety of occupations related to health science, a roundtable discussion with professionals working in these fields, and a mind-boggling list of other careers to consider when wanting to blend passion or talent in these areas with your life's work.

SECTION 2 explore your options

By now you probably have a fairly good understanding of the assets (some fully realized and perhaps others only partially developed) that you bring to your future career. You've defined key characteristics about yourself, identified special interests and strengths, examined your work values, and analyzed your basic work personality traits. All in all, you've taken a good, hard look at yourself and we're hoping that you're encouraged by all the potential you've discovered.

You should be ready by now to shift your focus to the workplace. For careers in health science, the workplace includes hospitals, medical centers and clinics, research laboratories, and other places devoted both to preventing injuries and diseases as well as diagnosing and treating them. It can even include schools, corporate offices, and television studios.

With more than 10 million people working in more than 200 different careers in this field, health care is one of the nation's largest and fastest growing industries. In fact, due to a virtual explosion of technological advances in health care and a population infused with more elderly people than ever before, experts are projecting a whopping 25.5 percent increase in the number of health care jobs between 2000 and 2010. That's good news for up-and-coming health care professionals equipped with solid training, credentials in their respective fields, and strong backgrounds in math, science, and communications.

In the following section, you'll find in-depth profiles of 35 health care-related careers. As you explore these (and other) careers in health science,

fyi Each of the following profiles includes several common elements to help guide you through an effective career exploration process. For each career, you'll find

- A sidebar loaded with information you can use to find out more about the profession. Professional associations, pertinent reading materials, the lowdown on wages and suggested training requirements, and a list of typical types of employers are all included to give you a broader view of what the career is all about.
- An informative essay describing what the career involves.
- Get Started Now strategies you can use right now to get prepared,

test the waters, and develop your skills.
- A Hire Yourself project providing realistic activities like those you would actually find on the job. Try these learning activities and find out what it's really like to be a . . . you name it.

You don't have to read the profiles in order. You may want to first browse through the career ideas that appear to be most interesting. Then check out the others—you never know what might interest you when you know more about it. As you read each profile, think about how well it matches up with what you learned about yourself in Section 1: **Discover You at Work**. Narrow down your options to a few careers and use the rating system

described below to evaluate your interest levels.

- **No way!** There's not even a remote chance that this career is a good fit for me. (Since half of figuring out what you do want to do in life involves figuring out what you don't want to do, this is not a bad place to be.)
- **This is intriguing.** I want to learn more about it and look at similar careers as well. (The activities outlined in Section 3: **Experiment with Success** will be especially useful in this regard.)
- **This is it!** It's the career I've been looking for all my life and I want to go after it with all I've got. (Head straight to Section 3: **Experiment with Success**.)

it may help to know that there are five basic directions or "pathways" related to the health care industry. Understanding these pathways provides other important clues about which direction might be best for you and can help you narrow down the options most closely aligned with your personal goals and ambitions. The five health science pathways include:

Therapeutic Services

According to experts associated with the U.S. Department of Education's Career Cluster Initiative, people who work in therapeutic services focus on changing the health status of a given patient over time. They work directly with patients to provide care, treatment, counseling, and health education information. These types of careers require varying degrees of specialized training and generally require certification or licensure by a national professional organization and/or state agency.

Therapeutic careers profiled in this book include acupuncturist, art therapist, athletic trainer, audiologist, chiropractor, dental hygienist, dentist, dietician, emergency medical technician, home health aide, kinesiotherapist, massage therapist, mortician, nurse, occupational therapist, optometrist, pharmacist, physical therapist, physician, physician assistant, and veterinarian.

Diagnostic Services

Diagnostic service professionals use tests and other evaluation tools to detect, diagnose, and treat diseases, injuries, and other physical conditions. Most diagnostic careers require at least an associate's or bachelor's degree as well as specialized training and certification.

Computed tomography technologist, cytotechnologist, electroneurodiagnostic technologist, forensic pathologist, medical technologist, nuclear medicine technician, and phlebotomist are examples of diagnostic professions that are profiled in this book.

Health Informatics

Health informatics covers all the administrative functions involved in health care, including the management of health care facilities, patient data, financial information, and computer applications. Depending on the position, training requirements vary from on-the-job training or certification to an associate's or bachelor's degree.

Careers in this pathway include admitting clerk, applied researcher, community services specialist, data analyst, ethicist, health educator, health information coder, health care administrator, patient financial services representative, medical librarian (or cybrian), patient advocate, public health educator, risk manager, social worker, transcriptionist, unit coordinator, and utilization manager. Epidemiologist, another important health informatics career, is profiled in this book.

A Note on Websites

Websites tend to move around a bit. If you have trouble finding a particular site, use an Internet browser to search for a specific website or type of information.

Support Services

Support services include functions necessary to ensure safe and efficient environments for the delivery of health care services. This pathway encompasses everything from cleaning and facility maintenance to food and transportation services. Career opportunities range from entry-level positions that require either on-the-job training or experience to technical and professional management positions that require advanced training.

Clinical technician, central services coordinator, environmental services technician, facility manager, food service personnel, maintenance engineer, materials manager, and transport technician are common types of support services occupations. This book includes a profile of an industrial hygienist.

Biotechnology Research and Development

Biotechnology research and development is an exciting and constantly evolving health care pathway. Primarily the domain of highly skilled scientists, this pathway involves researching new treatments and medicines for diseases as well as new diagnostic tools and tests. Key positions in this pathway require at least a bachelor's degree and many require a master's or doctoral degree. However, those looking to get started with less training may find opportunities as lab technicians and research assistants. Since biotechnology research and development professionals do not work directly with patients, they tend to work for universities and government agencies.

This book includes profiles of biochemist, bioinformatics scientist, geneticist, biomedical engineer, and microbiologist.

As you explore the individual careers in this book and others in this series, remember to keep what you've learned about yourself in mind. Consider each option in light of what you know about your interests, strengths, work values, and work personality.

Pay close attention to the job requirements. Does it require math aptitude? Good writing skills? Ability to take things apart and visualize how they go back together? If you don't have the necessary abilities (and don't have a strong desire to acquire them), you probably won't enjoy the job.

For instance, several popular TV shows make forensic investigation look like a fascinating career. And it is—for some people. But when considering whether forensic investigation—or any career for that matter—is right for you, think about the skills it takes to succeed. In this case, we're talking about lots of chemistry, anatomy, and physics. And, quite frankly, working with dead people. Be realistic about each profession so that you can make an honest assessment about how appropriate it is for you.

find your future

acupuncturist

acupuncturist Acupuncturists get right to the point of health care. That's because their healing procedures rely primarily on using needles—lots of them—to balance the body's energy flow. Acupuncture is based on an ancient Chinese theory that says a subtle energy system, called *qi* (pronounced "chee"), runs through the body. Much like blood in the circulatory system, qi circulates throughout the body through a "transportation" system that includes 14 meridians. When all is well, the energy flows freely, the body maintains its health, and systems function normally. When qi becomes blocked, any number of symptoms or illnesses can result.

Acupuncture is a tool used to restore the flow of qi. The process involves gently inserting tiny, sterile, flexible (and painless) needles at very specific points, called acupoints, along the meridians. There are hundreds of acupoints, each one associated with a specific organ or system. A trained acupuncturist uses the same types of diagnostic techniques that a medical physician uses—observation, examination, and questioning—to determine trouble spots. Using that information, the acupuncturist figures out which acupoints need attention. For instance,

---

Get Started Now!

- Enroll in anatomy and physiology classes to learn as much as you can about the human body.
- Visit an acupuncturist to see what the treatment is like. Discuss the acupuncturist's own career path with him or her.
- Browse through the alternative health section at your local library or bookstore and see what you can learn.
- Take a massage class to see how well you work with your hands.

Search It!
American Academy of Medical Acupuncture at *www.medicalacupuncture.org* and American Association of Oriental Medicine at *www.aaom.org*

Read It!
Alternative Health News Online at *www.altmedicine.com*

Learn It!
Specific requirements vary from state to state; however, many require a three- to four-year "master's level" degree from an accredited school. Find schools approved by the Council of Colleges of Acupuncture and Oriental Medicine at *www.ccaom.org*.

Earn It!
Earnings generally range from $20,000 to $70,000.
(Source: U.S. Department of Labor)

Find It!
Most acupuncturists are self-employed. Look in the phone book for private practices and alternative care centers.

Hire Yourself

Use resources such as the interactive acupuncture chart found at *www.qi-journal.com/tcmarticles/acumodel/ acumodel.asp* and other resources you find on-line or at the library to identify and describe the 14 meridians associated with acupuncture. Make a chart using your favorite computer resources or, if you prefer, markers and a large sheet of poster board.

a patient with nausea might be treated with needles inserted into specific acupoints on the wrist. Someone with a vision problem might be treated with needles inserted into acupoints in the feet.

Traditional doctors and scientists can't explain why acupuncture helps relieve illnesses. However, there is a growing body of evidence that supports the usefulness of acupuncture in treating or preventing various ailments such as allergies, arthritis, rheumatism, digestive problems, headaches and migraines, insomnia, and sinusitis. Acupuncture is now so widely accepted as an alternative form of medicine that most health insurance companies provide at least partial coverage for acupuncture treatments.

Although acupuncture itself hasn't changed much in the past 5,000 years, the way that acupuncturists are trained has. In the past, almost anyone could become an acupuncturist. All it took was a general idea of the process, a place to see patients, and a supply of needles. Today, acupuncturists have to go through rigorous training and often must complete three to four years in accredited acupuncture schools to become certified. Some acupuncturists also have a traditional medical degree and experience. And the training doesn't stop there: most acupuncturists complete an additional 100 hours of seminars and courses each year. With that said, it should come as no surprise that an in-depth knowledge of anatomy and health is essential for acupuncturists. So is a genuine desire to help people feel better.

Acupuncturists can set up shop just about anywhere. Some work out of a home-based office equipped with the necessary medical equipment. Many acupuncturists establish private practice offices or team up with other alternative medicine practitioners to open "holistic" health clinics. Currently, there are more than 10,000 acupuncturists practicing in the United States. Because reputable research studies continue to associate positive results with acupuncture, it's quite likely that this occupation will stick around for a while!

Search It!
American Art Therapy Association
at *www.arttherapy.org* and
American Dance Therapy
Association at *www.adta.org*

Read It!
*American Dance Therapy
Association Newsletter* at
www.adta.org

Learn It!
- Undergraduate degree in counseling or psychology
- Master's degree may be required
- Experience in fine arts

Earn It!
Median annual salary is $48,000.
(Source: American Art Therapy Association)

Find It!
Art therapists mostly work in hospitals and schools.

find your future
art therapist

art therapist

Art therapists use creativity to help clients get a handle on their emotional, social, or educational development. Through the use of artwork, dance, or music, these specialized therapists see the healing benefits of fine arts. Art, therapists believe, is a language with no barriers. Everyone can benefit from this type of therapy.

Like other therapists, art, music, and dance therapists talk to people about problems or stress. Art is like a prop. It prompts clients to speak up and express their emotions. A therapist who uses artwork, for example, analyzes a patient's drawings for hints about what's going on with his or her mental health. A therapist who uses dance can help a patient express feelings through dances like ballet or the cha-cha. And music therapists believe in the healing power of sound to help patients through difficult times.

In all of these fine art occupations, therapists usually work with patients on a one-to-one basis. Their goal is to get the patient to talk about their emotions and even to help ease the pain of serious illnesses such as acquired immunodeficiency syndrome (AIDS). During a session, therapists take detailed notes and keep track of the patient's progress. Therapists must be able to change the therapy to make it new and exciting. That's why imagination and creativity are key for art therapists.

Although anyone can benefit from this type of therapy, children and older adults are often the focus. A picture is worth a thousand words, and

Get Started Now!
- Volunteer at your local hospital, nursing home, or school for children with disabilities.
- Get involved in your school's art, music, or dance programs. It will expose you to different types of fine arts.
- Talk to a therapist in the field you're interested in. Ask if you can sit in on a session or participate in a group session.

Hire Yourself!

Art therapists often use colors to help patients understand and express their emotions. For example, yellow is a bright color that can help cheer you up. Red may mean anger, stress, or danger. What does your favorite color say about you? Use the Internet or library to research your top five colors. Make a color chart that lists the color and its effect on people or the environment.

that's especially true for young children or teens with language problems. Art therapy helps these kids express themselves without speaking. The same goes for older people who may be suffering from mental illness or a health problem that keeps them from talking. Art and music do wonders to help calm older patients or even boost their creativity.

Because therapists deal with several types of problems—like depression, paranoia, behavioral aggression, and severe anxiety—it's important for them to stay strong mentally. That can be challenging and tiring. Patients often need several years of weekly therapy. Inner strength, patience, and the desire to help others are major requirements for this career.

A love and understanding of the healing power of fine art is another obvious requirement. So is the ability to use psychology to understand people. Art therapists usually have a bachelor's degree in psychology, counseling, or a related field. Some therapists may even have their master's or doctorate. Plus, they are experienced fine artists and can teach artistic skills to people.

You can find art, music, or dance therapists working in hospitals, long-term care facilities such as nursing homes, and in schools. Most therapists own their own practice and are hired by these institutions to help patients. A 40-hour workweek is standard, but some therapists also work nights, weekends, and holidays to accommodate their patients.

Search It!
National Athletic Trainer's Association at **www.nata.org** and AthleticTrainer.com at **www. athletictrainer.com**

Read It!
Read current articles about the athletic training profession at **www.nata.org/industry resources/inthenews.htm**

Learn It!
Requires a four-year degree with a major in a medical or health science-related area, plus completion of an accredited certification program. Find links to accredited training programs at **www.cewl.com**.

Earn It!
Median annual salary is $33,650. (Source: U.S. Department of Labor)

Find It!
Chat with athletic trainers employed at local health clubs, corporations, and high schools, or look at postings for currently available athletic training positions at **www.athletictrainer.com**.

find your future athletic trainer

athletic trainer

Athletic trainers are part of an elite team of health care professionals. The focus of their job is enhancing the quality of health care available to athletes and other physically active people. Their work unfolds on athletic fields and in physical fitness facilities in high schools, colleges, universities, sports medicine clinics, and professional sports teams.

Regardless of where athletic trainers work, they all share three main responsibilities: preventing sports-related injuries, providing on-site injury care, and planning and managing injury rehabilitation programs. Of course, prevention is the preferred approach, which is why athletic trainers work diligently with coaches and individual athletes alike to make sure that every athlete is playing safely, as well as at his or her personal best. They provide training lectures on things like the importance of hydration and proper playing techniques. They stress the importance of good nutrition and emphasize the necessity of staying fit and strong. In many cases, they work one-on-one with individual athletes to develop personal training plans.

Get Started Now!

- Get involved in lots of recreational sports.
- If your school or health club has an athletic trainer on staff, volunteer to help out. As an assistant, you'll get the low-down on what the job entails—and get some key experience for the future.
- Enroll in sports management courses at school.
- Volunteer at a local hospital, clinic, or college health department. It'll help you learn the basics of treatment, while scoring big points with a future employer.
- Learn CPR, first aid, and other life-saving treatments. Contact your local American Red Cross office for information.

Hire Yourself!

Go for the gold! You're working towards certification as an athletic trainer and have been selected to interview for an apprenticeship with the U.S. Olympic Training Center. Part of your interview involves choosing any two of the sports included in the Olympic Games. Go on-line to *www.olympic.org/uk/sports/index_uk.asp* for a complete listing of resources related to each officially sanctioned sport. Use these resources, plus those found at the U.S. Olympic Training Center website at *www.olympic-usa.org* and any others you find on your own, to create a chart comparing three potential physical hazards associated with each sport. This might include risks associated with specific body parts such as shoulder injuries for a gymnast or knee injuries for a runner. It may include reference to special dietary needs such as high calorie diets for weightlifters and low calorie for swimmers. It may also include recommendations for specific types of exercise regimens that build bodies that can withstand the demands of world-class competition. Be prepared to explain the differences at your interview.

Whether it's football, soccer, wrestling, or cheerleading, athletic trainers create appropriate exercise programs for their clients. A high school basketball player, for example, can work with a trainer to improve his shot or his running endurance. Athletic trainers work one-on-one for specific problems. At the same time, they work with the entire team to make sure all are practicing and playing at their peak.

However, when it comes to sports, injuries happen. It's inevitable. That's why athletic trainers must be prepared with an impressive array of injury treatment skills. This is where all the training in subjects like anatomy, physiology, and even kinesiology come into play. Since there may even be times when an athletic trainer must provide emergency life-saving treatment, it's easy to understand why the certification process for athletic trainers is so rigorous—a four-year degree plus up to 800 hours of certification training and experience.

In addition, athletic trainers must stay alert to recognize potential problems among the athletes. Sometimes what seems like a minor ache or pain can, in reality, indicate a more serious problem. Other times, given the driven and competitive natures of many athletes, trainers must stay alert to unreported injuries so that no one bravely (and foolishly) ends up playing in spite of a painful injury.

Last, but not least, athletic trainers plan and implement rehabilitation regimens for athletes who are recovering from injuries. This again takes serious levels of medical know-how to administer correctly. Athletes' health and future physical well-being is at stake, so you want someone who knows what they're doing in charge of the recovery process.

A love of sports and fitness is a clear reason to become an athletic trainer. The desire for plenty of variety on a daily basis is also a bonus.

In a typical day, trainers do everything from working up a sweat in the gym to planning and presenting a variety of injury prevention lessons to monitoring the rehabilitation therapies of several athletes.

Another benefit that can be associated with athletic training: lots of travel. Trainers who work with pro teams get to trek around the globe along with the players. If you'd rather keep your feet close to home, don't worry. High schools, colleges, universities, even large corporations and health clubs, hire athletic trainers. Finding the right job as an athletic trainer should be no sweat!

find your future: audiologist

Search It!
Academy of Dispensing Audiologists at *www.audiologist.org*, the American Speech-Hearing-Language Association at *www.asha.org*, and the National Student Speech Language Hearing Association at *www.nsslha.org*

audiologist

Listen up! Audiologists care for people with all kinds of hearing problems ranging from hearing loss, tinnitus (noises in the ear), equilibrium disorders, and central auditory processing deficits. Audiologists treat patients ranging from brand new babies all the way to senior citizens. Whenever possible they diagnose and treat hearing problems with medication, therapy, or, under certain circumstances, surgery. In cases of severe hearing loss where nothing can be done to actually "heal" the patient, they develop rehabilitation plans that might include carefully prescribed hearing aids, amplification systems, or assistive listening devices.

Prevention of hearing loss is another big responsibility for audiologists. Many work in schools helping to detect early signs of hearing disorders in children. Others focus their efforts on corporate settings by providing prevention tools and counseling services for employees who are exposed to excessive noise in their workplaces.

Since speech and hearing are so closely intertwined, audiologists sometimes work with speech pathologists. When this happens their goal is to evaluate speech, language, and communication skills in order to help people make the most of their limited hearing capacity. In addition, audiologists often coordinate efforts with other health care professionals such as physicians, physical therapists, optometrists, and teachers.

Read It!
Hearing Health Magazine at *www.hearinghealthmag.com*

Learn It!
- Undergraduate degree with an emphasis on communication disorders or speech and hearing science
- Master's degree in audiology

Earn It!
Median annual salary is $48,400. (Source: U.S. Department of Labor)

Find It!
Seek out audiologists in schools, hospitals, clinics, colleges, and government health agencies.

Get Started Now!

- Talk to an audiologist about a typical day. You can find an audiologist in schools, doctor's offices, or clinics.
- Volunteer at a hearing clinic offered through your local health department.
- Take as many biology, health sciences, and mathematics courses as you can. The knowledge will help you in the future.

Hire Yourself!

Audiologists often work with children in an effort to prevent hearing problems through age-appropriate education programs. Your job is to pick a target audience—either kindergarten, elementary school, or middle school. Use information you find at the How Stuff Works website at *http://entertainment.howstuffworks.com/hearing.htm* to create a poster or game that helps your target audience better understand the hearing process.

Another part of an audiologist's job is to keep up-to-date on research, reports, and treatment methods. And, of course, there's the inevitable paperwork to keep on track. Since the medical field is constantly changing with new innovations and technologies, audiologists have to stay current in their field by reading journals and attending continuing education courses.

Besides having the commitment and ability to successfully acquire the required academic credentials, audiologists must also enjoy working closely with people. The ability to listen, troubleshoot problems, and communicate effectively are also important job requisites.

As for where audiologists work, many set up their own private practice while others work in a clinic or office with other doctors. Other audiologists work for public school systems, state agencies, hospitals, corporations, or research facilities.

Experts predict that audiologists will be in high demand throughout the coming decade. That's because an ever-increasing percentage of the U.S. population will be elderly. Since hearing loss is commonly associated with aging, this means that more people will be at risk for hearing loss.

find your biochemist future

biochemist

biochemist It can accurately be said that a biochemist is part scientist and part detective. Yes, biochemistry starts with the pure science of chemistry and biology. But scientific theory is just the starting point. Biochemists use science as a launchpad to solve problems related to any and all types of living organisms—from humans to animals to the tiniest of microbes.

Although many of the processes biochemists study are so minute they are invisible to the naked eye, the problems they attempt to solve can be huge. Developing new medicines, devising ways to safely treat and manage wastewater and pollutants, and researching carcinogenic (cancer-causing) toxins are just a few of the major world problems being tackled through biochemistry.

Biochemists study how substances, such as drugs, hormones, and food, impact humans and other forms of life. Some research how diseases attack cells, how to prevent it from happening, and how to treat it if it does happen. Others develop environmentally-friendly pesticides. Still other biochemists teach in universities and consult for government agencies. As you can probably tell, it's a broad field that encompasses many aspects of biology and chemistry.

Get Started Now!

- Eat, sleep, and breathe biology and chemistry. Keep up your grades and ask your teacher for extra lab work focusing on biochemistry principles.
- Take as much advanced math and science as you can manage. Without a strong foundation in high school, it's very hard, if not impossible, to catch up in college.
- Stay current with new developments in science by monitoring the science pages in major newspapers and on-line news sources such as CNN (*www.cnn.com*) and *Scientific American* (*www.scientificamerican.com*).

Search It!
American Society for Biochemistry and Molecular Biology at
www.asbmb.org

Read It!
Biochemical Journal at
www.biochemj.org/bj.htm and
The Biochemist at ***www.biochemist.org/news***

Learn It!
A bachelor of science degree in biochemistry is a minimum requirement, but many positions require a master's or doctorate.

Earn It!
Average annual salary is $60,390. (Source: U.S. Department of Labor)

Find It!
Biochemists work in laboratories and for chemical and pharmaceutical companies. Employers include Biogen at ***www.biogen.com*** and Hoffman-La Roche at ***www.rocheusa.com***.

Hire Yourself!

If you're like most American teens, you probably consume your fair share of junk foods. The problem with junk foods is that they tend to contain high levels of fat and almost non-existent levels of useful nutrients. How is it that something that tastes so good can be so bad for your body?

Your job as your school's resident biochemist is to find out. Start with what you learn about how fat works at the How Stuff Works website at *http://home.howstuffworks.com//fat.htm* and your own Internet investigation about the effect of fat on the human body, and prepare a clear and concise scientific bulletin warning your fellow students of the dangers of overindulging in fatty foods.

Have you ever taken a math or science course in school and wondered if what you were learning had anything to do with what you need to know to succeed in the real world? Biochemistry is one profession where you're bound to use everything you could possibly learn in math and science courses alike. Algebra—and statistics, arithmetic, geometry, trigonometry, and calculus, for that matter—is used almost daily. Familiar with the scientific method? You'll go nowhere in this profession without it.

People who like being part of a team of thinkers do well in this field. Biochemists often work with physiologists, pharmacologists, chemists, biologists, and other professionals, which is one reason why good communication skills are vital for success in this field. It's not enough to make brilliant discoveries—you have to be able to clearly explain those discoveries to others.

Good management and business skills are also a plus—especially as biochemists advance in the field and become responsible for supervising other lab assistants and scientists. Being an efficient and capable manager helps keep the lab functioning effectively. Along with managerial duties come budgeting duties. Biochemists often have to secure funding and grants for research projects. When federal or foundation grants are associated with a specific project, fiscal management is added to the job responsibilities.

Getting started as a biochemist requires a bachelor's degree in biochemistry. However, due to the complex nature of this type of work, many companies require biochemists to have a master's or doctoral degree. The extra schooling pays off: someone with an undergraduate degree can earn up to an average of $50,000; a master's degree gets you nearly $58,000. Biochemists with their doctorate rake in even more: over $73,000 on average.

According to labor experts, thousands of biochemistry jobs will open up in the next 20 years. Qualified candidates will be in high demand to fill vacancies and new positions in both private companies and government agencies, which makes this career a promising choice for aspiring scientists.

find your future

bioinformatics scientist

Search It!
National Center for Supercomputing Applications at *www.ncsa.uiuc.edu*, the National Bioinformatics Institute at *www.bioinfoinstitute.com*, and Northwest Alliance for Computational Science and Engineering at *www.nacse.org*

Read It!
data link newsletter at *www.ncsa.uiuc.edu/News/datalink*

Learn It!
● Bachelor's degree in biology or computer science plus a master's degree in bioinformatics
● Doctorate (Ph.D) is required for high-level positions

Earn It!
Average annual salary is $56,980. (Source: U.S. Department of Labor)

Find It!
Employers include Oscient Pharmaceuticals at *www.oscient.com* and the National Human Genome Research Institute at *www.genome.gov*

bioinformatics scientist

Interested in a career with importance comparable to landing on the moon, splitting the atom, or the invention of the wheel? A career in bioinformatics just might fit the bill for you. According to the Indiana University School of Informatics, bioinformatics is a "pure and applied science dealing with the collection, management, analysis, and dissemination of biological data and knowledge, especially with respect to genetics and molecular biology."

The profession is as cutting-edge as it gets and is still riding high from the spectacular uncovering of the human genome sequence in 2001. Bioinformatics is a complex and exciting field with the potential to discover cures for diseases such as AIDS, cancer, and most inherited diseases, and even provide solutions to health problems associated with

Get Started Now!
● Create your own webpage if you don't already have one. If you do have one, upgrade it with a new design or consider creating webpages for others. The experience will increase your knowledge of computers and programming language.
● Take high-level or advanced placement math and science courses.
● Enroll in computer programming courses at your school.
● Get inside the Human Genome Project at *www.genome.org*. In addition to learning about genetics, you may be able to scout out a bioinformatics scientist to email—a great opportunity to get an insider's view of the field.

Hire Yourself!

You work for a major genetics company and you're in need of a new bioinformatics scientist. Write a "help wanted" advertisement for the position. Include information about your company, qualifications for the applicants, a list of responsibilities they'll encounter, and the starting salary. Include bonuses, benefits, and whatever you think will entice specialists to apply. Use the Internet to run a search for *bioinformatic jobs* to compare your ad with what real employers are really looking for and offering. Make adjustments to your ad as necessary.

aging. It also shows great promise in the quest to improve genomes related to economically important crops and animals.

As you may have already guessed by now, it takes complex thinking to solve complex problems like these. Getting the education needed to succeed requires an interdisciplinary approach involving study in areas such as biology, computer science, chemistry, and library and information science. Proficiency in subjects like algebra, calculus, and statistics are good early indicators of the analytical minds best suited for this type of work.

Once on the job, bioinformaticians can expect to be involved in tasks like analyzing extremely large batches of data related to genomic science. Without the able assistance of very sophisticated technology and specialized software, this process could be likened to finding a needle in a haystack. Technology, however, provides the power to boldly go where no mind has ever gone before. Drawing inferences, developing new statistical methods for making sense of the data, finding answers to questions that have eluded mankind since the beginning of time—it's all in a day's work for bioinformatics scientists.

Bioinformatics is a field that's expected to grow by leaps and bounds in the coming years. Currently, there is a limited number of experienced bioinformaticians to fill rapidly growing vacancies in industry and government. This all adds up to one thing for aspiring scientists with an interest in exploring new frontiers of discovery—opportunity.

Search It!

The Whitaker Foundation at *www.whitaker.org*, Biomedical Engineer at *www.biomedicalengineer.com*, and International Federation for Medical and Biological Engineering at *www.ifmbe.org*

Read It!

Find access to all kinds of information and resources related to biomedical engineering at *www.bmenet.org/BMEnet*

Learn It!

- A bachelor's degree in biology, physics, or engineering
- A master's degree in engineering or biomedical engineering

Earn It!

Average annual salary is $60,410. (Source: U.S. Department of Labor)

Find It!

Major employers include Bristol-Myers Squibb Company at *www.bms.com*, Eli Lilly & Company at *www.lilly.com*, and Boston Scientific at *www.bostonscientific.com*.

find
biomedical
your engineer
future

biomedical engineer

Biomedical engineering combines three health and science jobs—biologist, researcher, and engineer—into one action-packed career. Thanks to biomedical engineers, people at risk for heart failure now have access to brilliantly engineered artificial hearts. Eyesight, in certain circumstances, can be restored through corrective eye surgeries made possible with advanced laser systems. People who have lost a limb or need hip or knee replacements now benefit from state-of-the-art biotic orthotics and prosthetics. And that's not all. Biomedical engineers design and develop new medical monitoring, diagnostic, and therapeutic equipment that solve all kinds of medical problems. These high-tech devices and procedures have saved the lives of many people and improved the lives of countless more.

Get Started Now!

- Like many medical and scientific professions, biomedical engineering requires a strong foundation of math and science. If you have even a remote sense that this type of work might be part of your future, you'll want to get started now by loading up on life sciences and advanced math courses.
- Hone your tone by participating in speech contests or your high school debate club.
- Make it a high school goal to learn to express yourself with clear, concise writing.
- Keep tabs on what's going on. Check the Internet and national news magazines for articles of interest. Mind-controlled biotics is one area to watch.

Hire Yourself!

You're working as a biomedical consultant and a doctor calls to ask for your help finding the best options for replacing the hand of a young patient. The patient is 10 years old and is very active. The doctor asks you to seek out three of the best options. Your job is to use the Internet to find out all you can about biotic hands. Use a search engine to conduct word searches for *biotic hands*, *prosthetics*, or *artificial limbs*. You can also research companies specializing in orthotics and prosthetics such as **www.ossur.com**.

Print out diagrams of the three products that you think will be most useful and attach a diagram of each to separate sheets of paper. Using product descriptions you find on-line, explain why you think each of these options may be appropriate for a young patient.

With recent advances in technological capabilities, there has been unprecedented growth in this field. The federal government makes a considerable investment in the field through research and funding opportunities made possible through the National Institute of Biomedical Imaging and Bioengineering. In addition, new biomedical companies have sprung up in record numbers, and health-related corporations are pouring huge amounts of energy and resources into researching and developing biomedical products. That's good news for future biomedical engineers. Experts say employment will increase faster than the average for all occupations through 2010.

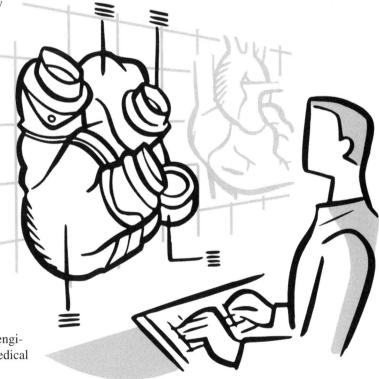

This is true particularly in light of America's aging population. As a general rule, older people tend to have more frequent and more complex medical problems. Bio-medical solutions are expected to address many of the common ailments associated with aging and to improve the overall quality of life for senior citizens. That said, it is safe to assume that biomedical engineers will be in high demand in the coming years.

Specialization within biomedical engineering is growing as well. Biomedical engineers who focus on rehabilitation, orthopedics, cellular engineering, vascular engineering, and medical imaging can look forward to a bright employment outlook.

New fields are constantly emerging too, like microbiotic surgery. Professionals in this specialty research and develop automated equipment and computer devices for surgery. Recently, a biomedical engineer and a biologist worked together to develop a tiny computerized machine that detects breast cancer tissue in mice. Researchers are closing in on the development of "mind-controlled" prosthetic devices—artificial limbs that will function in much the same way that real ones do. Imagine the implications this research will have on our world!

You may be surprised to learn that after all the requisite academic credentials and intellectual abilities, there are other critical on-the-job skills needed by biomedical engineers. Patience and imagination come in particularly handy. Patience, because the kinds of problems these professionals work on aren't solved overnight. Imagination, because they have to "think outside the box" in both complex and practical ways to solve the problems associated with their work. Communication skills—both verbal and written—are essential in order to accurately convey ideas to other scientists, medical professionals, and the general public. Of course, the big pay-off (besides generous salaries) comes with knowing that the result of this work is improving the quality of life for people everywhere.

chiropractor

When someone's neuro-musculoskeletal system is out of whack, a chiropractor's office is where they often go for help. Chiropractors are increasingly gaining respect as holistic health providers who use a hands-on integrative healing system to address ailments connected to the relationship between the body's structure (primarily the spine) and function (primarily the nervous system).

The main culprit affecting their patients, chiropractors will tell you, is a condition called subluxation. Subluxation describes any number of functional and structural changes in joints which interfere with nerve transmission, disturb other organ systems, cause pain or discomfort, and generally wreak havoc with a person's health and physical well-being.

Dr. Daniel David Palmer is credited with developing the basic principles behind chiropractic care in 1895. Although many refinements and improvements have been made in the field since then, chiropractors still

Get Started Now!

- Stack your schedule with science. Take as many biology, chemistry, and anatomy courses as you can.
- Consider visiting a chiropractor (with your parent's approval, of course). Many offer a free initial consultation where they explain the process and, if you explain your interest in the profession, they are likely to be happy to talk with you about it.
- Sign up for yoga or Pilates classes at your school (if offered) or local health club or check out a beginning yoga or Pilates video from your local library or video rental store. Both of these fitness programs focus on building strength and flexibility and will help you get acquainted with your own structural system.

Search It!
American Chiropractic Association at *www.amerchiro.org* and the Chiropractic Resource Organization at *www.chiro.org*

Read It!
ACA Today (electronic version) at *www.amerchiro.org/publications/aca_today.shtml* and *ChiroZine* at *www.chiro.org/ChiroZine*

Learn It!
- Two years of college, with a focus on science, biology, chemistry, and lab work
- Four years of specialized training in an accredited college (see *www.fclb.org/directory/index.htm*)

Earn It!
Median annual salary is $65,330. (Source: U.S. Department of Labor)

Find It!
Chiropractors usually open their own practice. Check your local phone book to investigate chiropractic services in your area.

Hire Yourself!

What does spinal misalignment have to do with bronchitis, pimples, and gout? Complete the following sequence of activities to find out.

First, go on-line to examine the spinal nerve chart at *www.drcurtisadams.com/spinal_nerve_chart.shtml*. Second, choose an ailment from the third column of the chart. Third, use your favorite search engine (such as *google.com* or *yahoo.com*) to run a search using the words *chiropractic* or *spinal subluxation* and the condition you chose. For instance, someone with an interest in the relationship between spinal misalignment and bronchitis would run a search using the words *spinal subluxation* and *bronchitis*. Finally, create a flowchart illustrating how chiropractors view the connection between the spine and the illness.

rely on the same natural, drugless, and nonsurgical practices as Dr. Palmer. In addition to diagnosing specific problems, chiropractors continue to emphasize the importance of nutrition, exercise, adequate rest, and safe environments as essential components of both recuperation from illness and a person's overall wellness.

A big part of a chiropractor's job is seeing patients to evaluate their spinal alignment. A slight tilt or imbalance in vertebrae, chiropractors believe, can eventually manifest itself through pain in the back, neck, shoulders, legs, hips, or head and aggravate other, seemingly unrelated, types of physical ailments.

Much like medical doctors, chiropractors examine patients and record medical histories to determine the problem. They may also take X rays or MRIs to get a look inside. Then, instead of drugs or surgeries, they use a combination of spinal adjustments or manipulations, massage, stretching exercises, heat therapy, water, light, and other alternative methods to get patients realigned and restored to good health.

Due to the hands-on approach of the chiropractic method, this type of health care can be physically demanding. Since they tend to spend the larger portion of the day examining and treating patients, chiropractors spend most of the day on their feet. However, most chiropractors have their own practice so they can set the hours that support their own physical needs. Eight-hour work days are typical, but so are evenings and weekends to accommodate patients.

Just one look around the hallway at a typical high school and you'll see why chiropractors are in high demand. With students lugging around 20 to 50 pound backpacks every day, it's no wonder the U.S. Bureau of Labor Statistics says chiropractic employment will grow faster than the average profession through 2010.

Of course, sports injuries are another source of consistent work for many chiropractors, some of whom focus primarily on sports medicine. Other chiropractic specialties include neurology, orthopedics, pediatrics, nutrition, internal disorders, and diagnostic imaging.

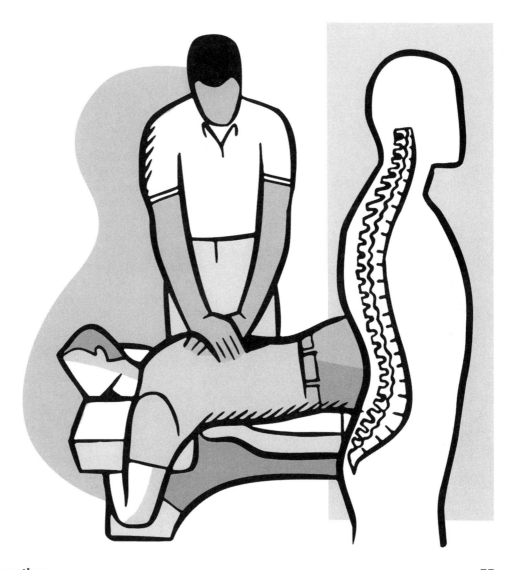

Search It!
American Society of Radiologic
Technologists at ***www.asrt.org***

Read It!
Journal of Electronic Imaging at
http://spie.org/app/Publications
and *Journal of Computer Assisted
Tomography* at ***www.jcat.org***

Learn It!
● Two-year degree, along with
specialized radiography certification provided through the
American Registry of Radiologic
Technologists (***www.arrt.org***)
● A four-year health science
degree along with certification in
radiology can be useful in purs-
ing advancement opportunities

Earn It!
Average annual salary for all types
of computed tomography positions
is $42,910. (Source: U.S.
Department of Labor)

Find It!
CT techs work in hospitals, radiology clinics, and X-ray clinics.

find *computed tomography your technologist future*

computed tomography technologist

Computed tomography technologists (CT techs) work with high-tech computers and special X-ray equipment to obtain very precise pictures of tissues, bones, and muscles that can be used in diagnosing injuries and diseases.

Using state-of-the-art diagnostic equipment is standard fare for computed tomographers. A CT scan system (also known as computed axial tomography or CAT scan) is their tool of choice. Multiple computers are used to control the entire CT system. The main computer that orchestrates the operation of the entire system is called the host computer. There is also a dedicated computer that reconstructs the raw CT data into an image. A workstation with a mouse, keyboard, and other dedicated controls allows the technologist to control and monitor the exam.

Get Started Now!

● Classes in biology, anatomy, and health help provide a solid foundation for this career.
● Contact a local hospital to ask about visiting a radiology clinic or hospital to observe CTs at work. Your high school guidance counselor or school-to-career counselor may be able to help line up this opportunity.
● Consider devoting part of your summer to volunteering at a local hospital. Many hospitals provide special training programs and opportunities for youth. Look on-line for information about hospitals near your home.

Hire Yourself!

Go on-line to How CAT Scans Work at *http://science.howstuffworks.com/cat-scan.htm*. Use the information you find here as well as other resources you find on your own to create a flowchart you could use to explain the CT scan process to patients.

This donut-shaped machine uses advanced X-ray technology to take pictures of cross-sections of a patient's body. These cross-sections are called *slices* and they provide views inside the brain and other parts of the body that cannot be seen on traditional X-ray equipment. While X rays provide flat, two dimensional pictures of bones and organs, CT scans reveal three-dimensional images that often provide life-saving early detection of diseases such as cancer and pulmonary embolisms.

The following list of duties, taken from an employment ad seeking certified CT techs, provides a glimpse of how these professionals interact with their patients and technology:

- Position and immobilize patient on examining table.
- Use supportive devices to obtain precise patient position.
- Follow instructions specified by the supervising radiologist to administer contrast media orally to patient (a harmless colored liquid ingested by patients that seeps into internal organs to provide better visibility on the scan).
- Enter data such as type of scan requested, slice thickness, scan time, and other technical data into computer.
- Start up CT scanner to scan designated anatomical area of patient.
- Talk to patient over intercom system and observe patient through window of control room to monitor patient safety and comfort.
- View images of organs or tissue on video display screen to ensure quality of pictures.
- Start camera to produce radiographs.
- Evaluate radiographs, videotape, and computer-generated information for technical quality.

This entire process takes anywhere from 15 to 30 minutes, depending on what needs to be done. Upon completion, the information is turned over to a radiologist for evaluation and diagnosis of any observable problems.

Physical strength and emotional compassion are especially useful skills for CT techs. Toned muscles come into play when lifting and positioning patients. The compassion is useful for helping calm patient fears about the procedure. Many people who undergo CT scans and other extensive radiology procedures have serious diseases or injuries and appreciate the efforts of health care professionals to care for them with sensitivity and dignity.

Interested in becoming a computed tomography technologist? Get ready to learn the ins and outs of using various radiology equipment. A two-year degree and a certificate in radiology will prepare you for starting out in this career. Many CT techs and other radiologic technologists later pursue a four-year degree as a way to open the door for more advanced opportunities. Some even go on to become medical doctors specializing in radiology.

find
cytotechnologist
your future

cytotechnologist

If cytology is the study of cells, what do you suppose cytotechnologists do? If you guessed that they "study cells" then you are 100 percent correct! Cytotechnologists examine human cell samples under microscopes, looking for early signs of cancer and other diseases. A skilled cytotechnologist can detect even the slightest abnormality in the color, shape, and size of the cell's cytoplasm and nucleus.

You can find cytotechnologists hard at work in laboratories or hospitals; they're the ones with microscope slides in their hands. Cytotechnologists cut, stain, and mount biological materials—like cells—on slides. Then they examine the specimens under a microscope and note what they see.

Their work is extremely important in identifying cancer and tracking its progress. Catching the illness in its early stages can make a huge difference for cancer patients. That's why it's absolutely critical for cytotechnologists to interpret cell changes correctly. An oversight

Search It!
American Society for Clinical Pathology at *www.ascp.org* and American Society for Cytotechnology at *www. asct.com*

Read It!
Histo-Logic technical bulletin at *www.sakuraus.com/ASPages/ Histo-Logic.asp* and *American Journal of Clinical Pathology* at *www.ajcp.com*

Learn It!
Bachelor's degree in science, plus a 12-month training program from a cytotechnology school

Earn It!
Average annual salary for cytotechnologists is $48,920. (Source: U.S. Department of Labor)

Find It!
Cytotechnologists work for large research hospitals, universities, and private laboratories. To find employers in your area, run an Internet search for *cytology research laboratory* in your state.

Get Started Now!

- Perfect the science of cutting, staining, and mounting slides. Ask your biology or chemistry teacher for help.
- Volunteer for national or regional cancer organizations, such as the American Cancer Society at *www.cancer.org* or the Susan G. Komen Breast Cancer Foundation at *www.komen.org*.
- Enjoy some quiet time. If you're always chatting and on the go, learn to slow it down. Spend some time alone and pay attention to your feelings and surroundings. It's good practice for a future career in cytology.

Hire Yourself!

A cytotechnologist can never know too much about the human cell. Brush up on your cellular know-how by going on-line to *www.enchantedlearning.com/subjects/anatomy/brain/label/neuron.shtml*. At this website you'll discover an opportunity to label the parts of a cell and check your answers on-line. Once you have everything labeled correctly, print out your chart and use it as a blueprint to create a three-dimensional model of a cell. Get creative in your use of materials and create a model that accurately portrays the various components of a healthy human cell.

or incorrect diagnosis can literally mean the difference between life and death.

After examining cell samples, cytotechnologists write up an evaluation and report their findings to the physician in charge. When abnormal cells are suspected, the cytotechnologist reports the findings to a pathologist who in turn examines the slide and issues a final report to the patient's physician.

Since cytotechnologists spend most of their time working over a microscope or writing reports, contact with patients is limited. People who work best independently make good cytotechnologists. That also means cytotechnologists are ultimately responsible for their own work. Having strong concentration skills is key, so cytotechnologists must have the ability to block out anything else that's going on around them. If you prefer working in a social setting with a group, this may not be the best profession for you. Although advanced cytotechnologists may train or supervise staff, that's not the reality for most.

To gear up for this career, you'll need a strong grip on biology in high school. College preparation includes a full load of science classes, and some colleges even offer bachelor's degrees in cytotechnology. After graduation, scientists head off to cytotechnology school for another year of specialized training and then must pass exams to enter the field.

find your dental hygienist future

dental hygienist

Dental hygienists are a smile's best friend. They're generally the first person a patient sees when visiting a dentist. Once a patient is in the dental chair, a hygienist begins by conducting a preliminary examination of the patient's teeth, sometimes taking X rays, and preparing laboratory tests for the dentist to use in assessing the condition of the patient's teeth and detecting any problems. Although dental hygienists may not actually diagnose dental diseases themselves, their preparatory work makes it possible for dentists to accurately and efficiently diagnose dental problems.

Next, the hygienist begins a thorough cleaning of the patient's teeth. This process includes using a variety of dental instruments and tools to remove plaque and stains from the teeth and, in some cases, applying fluoride treatments and sealants. Most dentists recommend that patients come in for this type of treatment at least two times each year.

While dentists spend most of their time correcting problems with patients' teeth, a dental hygienist's top priority is preventing problems. That's why a big part of a dental hygienist's job involves educating patients about proper oral hygiene. Hygienists are always ready to demonstrate the best way to brush and are generally more than willing to share a brief lecture about the benefits of flossing.

Get Started Now!

- Successful completion of high school courses in health, biology, psychology, chemistry, and speech can be useful in gaining acceptance into accredited training programs.
- Some high schools offer dental assisting programs. Find out about cooperative education opportunities through your local community college or technical school.
- Brush up on your dental hygiene. Haven't been to the dentist lately? Make an appointment and be sure to talk to the hygienist about his or her career.

Search It!
American Dental Hygienists' Association at *www.adha.org* and American Dental Assistants Association at *www. dentalassistant.org*

Read It!
Dental Angle magazine at *www.dentalangle.com*

Learn It!
- Two-year associate's degree in dental hygiene
- See *www.ada.org/prof/ed/ programs/search_dahlt_us. asp* for a list of accredited training programs

Earn It!
Average wage is $26.59 per hour. (Source: U.S. Department of Labor)

Find It!
Dental hygienists work in dental offices with general dentists and dental specialists such as orthodontists. Before you start job hunting, take a look at the tips featured at *www.adha.org/careerinfo/ jsearch/jsearch1.htm*.

Hire Yourself!

Use the oral health resources found on-line at *www. adha.org/careerinfo/jsearch/jsearch1.htm* to learn all you can about good dental habits. Then, incorporate what you've learned onto note cards that you can use for a five-minute presentation to share with your first patient.

In some dental offices, dental hygienists also work side-by-side with the dentist during dental procedures and surgeries, assisting with equipment and procedures. In some instances, these responsibilities are assumed by a specially designated and trained dental assistant, while in others it's part of the hygienist's list of duties.

In either case, this type of work involves equal measures of both technical and interpersonal skills. Since dentist visits often rank high on lists of things people most dread to do, keeping people physically and emotionally comfortable is an important (and especially appreciated) part of the job.

Starting out in this field requires a two-year college program focused on dental hygiene. To obtain a license after completing the course, hygienists must pass a written and clinical exam given by the American Dental Association. For those with aspirations beyond the dentist office—in career options such as dental research, marketing, sales, or teaching—a bachelor's degree in dental hygiene may be required.

Since this line of work is projected to be one of the 30 fastest-growing occupations in the coming years, qualified dental hygienists can expect to encounter plenty of opportunities to keep America smiling brightly. Flexible hours, comfortable work environments, and job stability are appealing factors often associated with this occupation.

find your dentist future

dentist

dentist Dentists are consistently listed among the top 10 most trusted and ethical professions in America, according to the American Dental Association. This distinction says a lot about the profession and the people who pursue it.

A typical day for a dentist involves seeing patients to fill cavities and diagnose and treat oral diseases and injuries. Dentists also perform oral surgeries, pull teeth, fit dentures, and use dozens of different instruments to treat—and prevent—a wide variety of problems. In recent years, dentists have also started offering cosmetic services such as whitening and capping to keep teeth looking as good as they feel.

Tools of the trade include drills, mouth mirrors, probes, forceps, brushes, and scalpels. Advances in technology such as digital radiology and laser systems are providing exciting new tools that enable dentists to work more effectively and efficiently.

Since most dentists work in private practices, their responsibilities also include overseeing a variety of administrative tasks such as hiring and training employees, purchasing equipment and supplies, marketing, and bookkeeping. However, for most dentists, the opportunity to be their own boss offsets time required to handle these types of responsibilities.

Get Started Now!
- Take college prep classes in biology, chemistry, and algebra.
- Look into dental assisting courses to give you a greater understanding of dental health.
- Volunteer to pitch in at community dental clinics or a local dentist's office.

Search It!
American Dental Association at **www.ada.org** and American Medical Association at **www.ama-assn.org**

Read It!
Dental Angle magazine at **www.dentalangle.com**

Learn It!
- Four-year college degree in biology, chemistry, or physics
- Four years at dental school. For information about accredited training programs, go to **www.dental-resources.com/dented2.html**

Earn It!
Median annual salary is $123,210. (Source: U.S. Department of Labor)

Find It!
Most dentists own their own practice or work in an office with other dentists. Some dentists also work in hospitals or for the military. Find information about the U.S. Army's dental care system at **www.dencom.army.mil/home.asp**.

Hire Yourself!

Getting new patients is a challenge for dentists. They have to find a way to attract—and keep—patients. Imagine you are a new dentist in your community. Create a newspaper advertisement or flyer to attract patients. You can focus on your schooling, a specialty, your personality, your office, tools and equipment, or anything else you can think of that will bring people to your door. You may look through the local phone book or newspaper for inspiration, but make certain that your ad is uniquely yours.

Although most dentists are general practitioners who see all kinds of patients for a variety of dental needs, one in nine dentists practice in specialty areas, including

- orthodontics—straightening teeth with braces or retainers
- oral and maxillofacial surgery—performing operations on the mouth and jaws
- pediatric dentistry—treating children
- periodontics—treating gum disease and the bones supporting the teeth
- prosthodontics—replacing missing teeth with permanent fixtures such as bridges or crowns and removable fixtures such as dentures
- endodontics—performing root canal therapies

People skills are essential for success in this field. Most people find it hard enough to endure having someone poking around their mouths with dental picks and drills. A sensitive, gentle dentist goes a long way to ensure that the experience is as pleasant—or at least as tolerable—as possible.

Like medical school, gaining admission into dental school is a very competitive process. That's why it's important to keep grades up during high school and college. Completing the requisite four years of dental training beyond the four years of undergrad work is also expensive.

However, the financial investment often pays off. Dentists who have their own practice can earn upwards of $150,000 per year. A dental specialist, like an orthodontist or an oral surgeon, can earn $250,000 or more. In fact, a dentist's income ranks in the highest 5 percent of family income earned in the United States.

And the news is good for prospective dentists. Since large numbers of dentists are expected to retire within the next 20 years, the job outlook is particularly favorable for newly credentialed dentists.

find your dietician future

dietician

Dieticians plan food and nutrition programs and prevent and treat illness through healthy eating and diet modification. Some dieticians obtain board certification as a specialist in renal nutrition (working with the maturational aspects of managing kidney transplantation, dialysis, or education about kidney disease) or as a specialist in pediatric nutrition (helping infants, children, and their families directly, or creating educational programs for them).

Childhood obesity is a national health epidemic that many dieticians are trying to address. While many countries (and some parts of the United States) have huge problems with lack of food, the leading health researchers in the United States have identified obesity as our number one nutrition problem. Estimates are that more than half of all adults are overweight, with a third being obese, and as many as 20 percent of all children are obese. In fact, the Commission of Dietetic Registration has just created the certificate of training in childhood and adolescent weight management to identify dieticians who are especially trained for this area.

Clinical dieticians work in hospitals, nursing homes, and correctional facilities. They educate patients about nutrition and work with the med-

Get Started Now!

- Take classes in biology, chemistry, and math.
- Keep a record of your own nutrition. Write down absolutely everything you eat for one week and tally your nutritional intake for each day. You can get information on most foods from the labels of packaged food, from the U.S. Department of Agriculture (*www.nal.usda.gov/fnic*), and from the websites of restaurant chains.
- Talk with your school or school district dietician about what his or her job is like.

Search It!
The American Dietetic Association at *www.eatright.org* and Commission on Dietetic Registration at *www.cdrnet.org*

Read It!
Dietician Central at *www.dietitiancentral.com* and UDSA Food and Nutrition Information Center at *www.nal.usda.gov/fnic*

Learn It!
- Registered dieticians (RDs) must complete a minimum of a bachelor's degree
- Dietician technicians, registered (DTRs) need to complete a minimum of a two-year associate's degree

Earn It!
Median annual salary is $41,170. (Source: U.S. Department of Labor)

Find It!
Find out what kind of opportunities are available for dieticians at *www.dieticianjobs.com*.

Hire Yourself!

Create a poster designed to encourage children and teens to have a healthy body image and eat a balanced diet. Make sure that you emphasize steering them away from fad diets and fast food and nudge them toward the good stuff. Be clear about the benefits of eating right and enthusiastic in presenting nutritional eating habits as the "cool" thing to do.

ical team to coordinate medical and nutritional needs for each patient. In small institutions, they may also manage the food service department.

Community dieticians work in public health clinics and health maintenance organizations (HMOs). They counsel individuals and groups on nutritional practices to prevent disease and promote good health. Some work for home health agencies, where they provide instruction of shopping and food preparation to the elderly and to individuals with special needs.

Management dieticians oversee large-scale meal planning and preparation in company cafeterias, prisons, and schools. In addition to nutritional expertise, they need to have experience in general management (hiring, financial management, reporting, and legal compliance).

Consultant dieticians have their own practice or work under contract with health care facilities. They may advise on the company cafeteria, design overall corporate wellness programs, or address specific concerns like weight management or cholesterol reduction. Some work with athletes or sports teams, helping players maintain the ideal weight for their sport in a healthy way. In private practice, they may work with eating disorders (anorexia, bulimia, obesity) or help people accommodate illnesses that respond to dietary changes (diabetes, cancer).

Dieticians who work in the corporate area may help food companies in product development and marketing, provide information for the company's website, or answer questions from customers. Some may have regular segments on television or radio shows, explaining new findings in nutrition to the public.

Research dieticians work for food and pharmaceutical companies, hospitals, and universities helping to answer questions about the relationship between food and health and finding alternative foods and processes.

find
electroneurodiagnostic technologist
your future

electroneurodiagnostic
technologist

Electroneurodiagnostic (END) technologists use a variety of techniques and sophisticated equipment to obtain interpretable recordings of the electrical activity of patients' brains and nervous systems. You did know that the brain and nervous system emit tiny electrical signals, didn't you? These electrical signals influence everything from human behavior to a person's sleep patterns. They also provide important data that can be used by doctors to diagnose injuries and diseases that affect the brain, spinal cord, central nervous system, and other parts of the body.

There are four electroneurodiagnostic procedures commonly conducted by END technologists. The most widely known is the electroencephalogram (EEG), a test that measures electrical activity in the brain and is especially useful in diagnosing brain-related problems such as head injuries, comas, strokes, epilepsy, and migraine headaches.

The evoked potential (EP) technique records electrical activity emitted from the brain, spinal nerves, or sensory receptors in response to external stimuli. This technique is used to scrutinize spinal injuries and monitor diseases such as multiple sclerosis.

Search It!
American Society of Electroneurodiagnostic Technologists (ASET) at *www.aset.org* and American Association of Electrodiagnostic Medicine at *www.aaem.net*

Read It!
Read the American Medical Association's description of this career at *www.ama-assn.org/ ama/pub/category/10481.html*

Learn It!
- Either a 12-month certificate or two-year associate's degree
- For a list of accredited training programs go to the education section of the ASET site at *www.aset.org*

Earn It!
Average annual salary is $36,430. (Source: U.S. Department of Labor)

Find It!
END technologists work in hospitals, research laboratories, and diagnostic testing clinics such as Duke University Medical Center at *www.mc.duke.edu*.

Get Started Now!
- Take courses in biology and anatomy. You'll learn the basics about the brain and nervous system.
- Find out about volunteer opportunities in your local hospital or medical center.
- Ask a teacher or guidance counselor to help arrange a visit to a neurologist's office or the neurology department of a local hospital where you can observe an END technologist conducting a variety of diagnostic tests.

Hire Yourself!

END Technologists perform four main kinds of diagnostic techniques:

- electroencephalography (EEG)
- evoked potential (EP)
- polysomnography (PSG)
- nerve conduction studies (NCS)

Take your pick of one of these tests and use your favorite Internet search engine (e.g., google.com or yahoo.com) and library resources to find out all you can about the technology, the procedure, and the medical uses of the technique. Report your findings in a brief PowerPoint presentation or chart.

Polysomnograms (PSGs) are used to evaluate sleep disorders and actually monitor many different activities including brain waves, eye movements, muscle activity, heartbeat, blood oxygen level, and respiration.

In addition, nerve conduction studies (NCS) are used to measure how long it takes nerve impulses to reach the muscle. This diagnostic tool is especially useful for investigating conditions such as carpal tunnel syndrome.

No matter which of these tests they use, END technologists follow similar procedures with each patient. For instance, suppose a patient arrives to be tested for breathing problems that his doctor suspects are occurring while he sleeps. The first thing the END would do is take some time to get acquainted with the patient, and question the patient about the nature of his symptoms. Next, the END would describe the procedure and prepare the patient for the actual test. During the test itself, the technologist would keep busy recording the data, calculating results, and maintaining the equipment. The END also would do whatever he or she can to assure the patient's comfort for the duration of the procedure—which can last anywhere from 20 minutes for a simple test to eight hours for an overnight sleep study. Finally, the END technologist would carefully compile the resulting data in a report for the consulting physician.

According to the American Society of Electroneurodiagnostic Technologists, the people most likely to succeed in this career have "actively inquiring minds, above average intelligence, and a willingness to engage in lifelong learning." By the year 2005, it will be necessary to have at least an associate's degree to qualify for positions in this field.

find your future
emergency medical technician

Search It!
National Association of Emergency Medical Technicians at
www.naemt.org

Read It!
EMS Magazine at ***www.emsmagazine.com***

emergency medical technician

If you've ever watched *Third Watch*, *ER*, or any other emergency room TV series, you probably have a good idea of what emergency medical technicians (also known as EMTs or paramedics) do. In real life, as on TV, EMTs often face some pretty dramatic situations. To say that their work can mean the difference between life and death is not an overstatement.

Quick and competent are the two qualities most widely appreciated in EMTs. With sirens blaring, or propellers whizzing in the case of flight-for-life EMTs, paramedics are often first on the scene of an emergency situation or accident. Through fast thinking and well-trained actions they often provide a vital lifeline for people with serious injuries or ailments. Their job is to evaluate and provide front-line treatment to minimize damage and sustain life while transporting the injured or ailing to a medical facility.

Although trained to provide immediate emergency care in situations involving bleeding, fractures, cardiac arrest, respiratory failure, and even childbirth, EMTs work closely with medical personnel to provide the best

Learn It!
- High school diploma or GED
- Completion of state certification process
- Registration with the National Registry of Emergency Medical Technicians (in most states). See ***www.nremt.org*** for details

Earn It!
Median annual salary is $24,030. (Source: U.S. Department of Labor)

Find It!
Opportunities are available in hospitals, local fire and police departments, private ambulance services, and independent emergency services companies. Check the Internet or telephone directory for employers near you.

Get Started Now!
- Get certified in cardiopulmonary resuscitation (CPR) and other life-saving techniques.
- Volunteer at your local EMT department, fire department, police department, or hospital.
- Ask to tag along with an EMT during a night or weekend shift.
- Take as many science courses as you can, including biology, health science, and nursing courses if they're available.

Hire Yourself!

Imagine that you've been newly certified as an EMT. It's your first day on the job and the first call has come in to rescue a 10-year-old boy who has been bitten by a venomous snake. Use Internet and library resources to find out what you must do to save his life. Use index cards to describe and illustrate each and every step involved in this type of life-threatening emergency.

possible support in any medical emergency. Via radio contact, EMTs convey important information about vital statistics and pre-existing conditions. That information helps hospital personnel provide guidance as necessary while the patient is still en route and enables them to make timesaving preparations to begin treatment as soon as the patient arrives.

Training to become an EMT varies from state to state. However, most states adhere to guidelines similar to those established by the National Registry of Emergency Medical Technicians (NREMT). Under NREMT guidelines, EMTs are ranked according to four levels of proficiency.

An EMT-Basic (EMT-1) is trained to provide emergency care and to transport injured patients to medical facilities under the direct supervision of medical personnel. The EMT-1 training includes learning to assess patient injuries and to manage respiratory, cardiac, and trauma emergencies.

Two levels are included in the EMT-Intermediate (EMT-2 and EMT-3) designation, in which EMTs are trained to administer intravenous fluids, use manual defibrillators, administer advanced airway techniques on patients in respiratory distress, and apply lifesaving shocks to heart attack victims.

Level Four (EMT-4) training results in the official classification of EMT-Paramedic. Paramedics must demonstrate competency in all Level One through Level Three procedures and are also trained to administer medications, interpret electrocardiograms, perform endotracheal intubations, and use monitors and other sophisticated equipment.

Needless to say, staying cool under pressure is a necessary prerequisite at all levels. So is being physically fit in order to accommodate the sometimes daunting physical demands of the job. EMTs spend lots of time kneeling, bending, lifting, and standing. They should be able to carry at least 100 pounds. EMTs typically work between 40 and 50 hours per week and are often on call for additional hours—just in case something comes up that requires their able assistance. As you've probably seen on TV and heard about in real life, EMTs often put their own lives on the line in order to save others.

Mental toughness is another necessity. This is a profession that deals with life and death on a daily basis. EMTs sometimes experience incredible highs after successfully resuscitating a heart attack victim or delivering a baby. But they also experience incredible lows when death or the results of violent crime are involved. They need to learn to strike a balance between human compassion and emotional detachment in order to handle the demands of their work.

Job prospects look good in this field. Employment opportunities are expected to grow faster than average through 2012 due to a growing population, increased funding for paid EMT positions, and a growing reliance on the care and protection these professionals provide for their communities.

Search It!
International Society for Environmental Epidemiology at *www.iseepi.org* and Epidemiologist.com at *www.epidemiologist.com*

Read It!
American Journal of Epidemiology at *www.aje.oupjournals.org*, *Emerging Infectious Diseases* at *www.cdc.gov/ncidod/EID/index.htm*, and Virtual Library of Epidemiology at *www.epibiostat.ucsf.edu/epidem/epidem.html*

Learn It!
- Bachelor's degree in chemistry or biology
- Master's and doctorate in a specialized area such as public health

Earn It!
Median annual salary is $53,840. (Source: U.S. Department of Labor)

Find It!
A major employer of epidemiologists is the Centers for Disease Control and Prevention at *www.cdc.gov*.

epidemiologist

A good way to understand what epidemiologists do is to think of them as disease detectives. Using a unique blend of high-tech tools, scientific know-how, and ample measures of common sense, their job is to solve the mysteries behind infectious and chronic diseases—whenever and wherever they occur. Unraveling these medical mysteries involves three main steps: figuring out the source of the disease; determining how the disease spreads from person to person; and, most challenging of all, discovering ways to stop and prevent further outbreaks of the disease.

Unlike other types of health professionals, epidemiologists do not work to improve the health of individual patients. Instead they focus on entire communities or even the world at large as they seek to understand and contain diseases such as cancer, acquired immunodeficiency syndrome (AIDS), severe acute respiratory syndrome (SARS), and even the ever present common cold. Recent world events have also brought a new sense of urgency to epidemiological research to be able to respond to chemical and biological terrorism.

Preparation for a career in this field depends largely on building a strong foundation in science and math. It's essential to begin laying the

Get Started Now!
- Contact your local health department (or go on-line to your state health department's website) and ask for information about the epidemiological efforts in your county.
- Get off to the right start by taking as many biology, chemistry, and mathematics courses as possible.
- Stay current with news reports concerning current efforts in the fight against diseases such as AIDS, cancer, and SARS.

Hire Yourself!

SARS is a disease that caused a worldwide stir when it first erupted in 2003. Go on-line to the Centers for Disease Control at *www.cdc.gov/ncidod/sars* to find information about the history and current status of this disease. Use the data that you discover to create a timeline tracing the first reported case to the ultimate containment of the disease.

groundwork in high school with a variety of honors and AP-level courses in subjects like biology, chemistry, and mathematics. The next phase involves pursuing a bachelor's degree in biology or chemistry. Additional training in a discipline such as public health is eventually required for professional development and advancement purposes.

In some ways, investigating diseases can be even more dangerous than investigating criminals. The "bad guys" epidemiologists go after may not even be visible to the naked eye, but they can be lethal all the same. The culprit could be a contaminated water source, a deadly microorganism, or even a killer mosquito or mouse. Some diseases are so contagious that it only takes one instance of unprotected contact with an infected person to contract it. To protect themselves epidemiologists are always equipped with gloves, gowns, and masks, or, in extreme cases, astronaut-like protective gear.

Epidemiologists are just as likely to be found working in a remote village in some far corner of the world as they are in a sterile, state-of-the-art laboratory. Epidemiologists go where the diseases are and, on really good days (sometimes after years of work), uncover cures to the most dreaded diseases known to humankind.

KEEP OUT!
QUARANTINE

Search It!
American Academy of Forensic
Sciences at **www.aafs.org** and
American Society for Investigative
Pathology at **www.asip.org**

Read It!
*Young Forensic Scientists Forum
Newsletter* at **www.aafs.org/
yfsf/index.htm** and the FBI's
Handbook of Forensic Services at
**www.fbi.gov/hq/lab/handbook/
intro.htm**

Learn It!
● Undergraduate degree in pre-
  med, plus four years or more in
  medical school
● Two to three years of specialized
  pathology education

Earn It!
Median annual salary is $184,000.
(Source: U.S. Department of Labor)

Find It!
For a sampling of currently available positions go on-line to
www.sciencejobs.com and run
a search for forensic jobs.

find your future forensic pathologist

forensic patholgist

Understanding what forensic pathologists do starts with a quick trip to the dictionary. There you'll discover that the word *forensic* is Latin in origin and means public and that pathology is the study of disease. Put the two words together and tweak it just a bit and you'll get the American Academy of Forensic Sciences' official definition: forensic pathology is the application of the principles of pathology, and of medicine in general, to the legal needs of society.

Did we mention that forensic pathologists work primarily with dead people? They perform autopsies to determine the causes of death when they occur under suspicious or unusual circumstances. If you've watched shows like *CSI, Quincy,* or *Crossing Jordan,* you've seen examples of this type of work in relation to violent deaths by homicide, suicide, or accident. While this is certainly part of the job, forensic pathologists also investigate the sudden deaths of seemingly healthy people, people who died from complications of medical treatment or procedures, and other types of suspicious situations. In some cases, the goal is simply to determine how and why someone died. In others it is to gather evidence that can be used in a criminal trial.

The primary function of forensic pathologists is to perform autopsies, but they also work with other types of forensic scientists such as criminologists who collect and examine physical evidence such as fibers from clothing. Toxicologists also add their expertise to the process by analyzing specimens of blood, urine, body tissues, and even the contents of the

Get Started Now!
● Take courses in biology, psychology, chemistry, and law.
● Watch forensic science shows on TV to get a general idea of what working in the field is like (minus all the glamour and romance, of course).
● Search a bookstore or library for books on forensics.

Hire Yourself!

What exactly is an autopsy? Go on-line to the American Medical Association's website and find their very informative on-line booklet *Autopsy: Life's Final Chapter* at *www.ama-assn.org/ama/pub/category/7635.html*. Use the information you find there and through other resources to create a flowchart that illustrates what the process involves from beginning to end.

deceased person's stomach for clues about the presence of alcohol, drugs, or other chemicals. Sometimes even forensic odontologists (dentists) are needed to help identify unknown deceased people.

While a good deal of a forensic pathologist's work generally takes place in a sterile laboratory, they often begin a new case at the actual scene of the death. This way they can gain firsthand information and clues about the circumstances of the death. Some of their work, such as preparing reports and managing paperwork, is done in an office. In addition, forensic pathologists spend time in courtrooms where they are asked to testify about their findings in certain cases.

Forensic pathology is a very specialized medical specialty. It takes years of rigorous training to qualify for the job. The training starts with a bachelor's degree in pre-med followed by four years of medical school. Specialized training in pathology comes next followed by an internship and a state certification process.

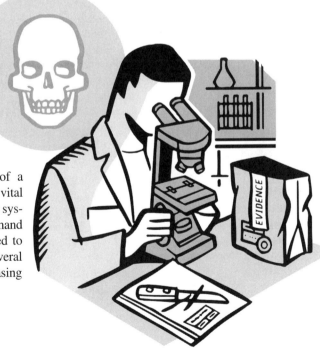

The work essentially blends the work of a physician, a detective, and a coroner and is a vital component of both the medical and the justice systems. Although there will never be a huge demand for forensic pathologists, the field is expected to grow faster than average over the next several years due to a growing population and increasing use of forensic testimony in court cases.

Search It!
National Society of Genetic Counselors at ***www.nsgc.org***, Genetics Society of America at ***www.genetics-gsa.org***, and the Institute for Genomic Research at ***www.tigr.org***

Read It!
Genetics at ***www.genetics.org*** and DNA from the Beginning at ***www.dnaftb.org***

Learn It!
- Bachelor of science in biology or genetics
- Doctorate in clinical genetics

Earn It!
Median annual salary is $61,470.
(Source: U.S. Department of Labor)

Find It!
Find career information for major companies like Applera at ***www.applera.com/applera/careers.nsf***, Qiagen at ***www.qiagen.com***, and the National Human Genome Research Institute at ***www.genome.gov/Careers***.

geneticist

Do you have your mother's blue eyes? Or your dad's dark hair? Or are you the spitting image of your grandmother when she was your age? What you look like is influenced by your genes. Geneticists study genes and genetic make-up of humans, animals, and plants. Their work helps us understand how certain traits are inherited.

Genetics is especially hot in the medical world right now due to a recent incredible breakthrough. In 2001, scientists completed mapping the human genome, a feat that's roughly the equivalent of uncovering nature's blueprint for building a human being. Now that geneticists know exactly what they're working with, their research is honing in on the functions of each individual gene and the role that faulty genes play in disease. The result of this continuing work is expected to lead to important discoveries in all aspects of health care including the diagnosis of diseases and improved treatments for diseases. Can you imagine the effectiveness of medications that are based on highly specific gene sequencing and structure? What about drugs that are customized to accommodate a patient's unique genetic profile? The possibilities are endless and very promising.

While some geneticists continue to focus on humans, others direct their efforts toward food. Geneticists who focus on agriculture help farmers produce larger and heartier crops. For instance, geneticists can

Get Started Now!
- Focus on science courses while in high school and load up on biology and hands-on lab courses.
- Take psychology or sociology courses, or read books pertaining to these two fields.
- See a virtual genetics museum exhibit from the American Museum of Natural History at ***www.amnh.org/exhibitions/genomics***.

Hire Yourself!

Each day, scientists make more advances in the field of genetics. With each advance, new ethical, religious, and social implications follow. When it comes down to it, geneticists—and people in general—are guided by their ethical beliefs. Geneticists walk a fine line between their moral values and the common good genetic research can provide. As a geneticist, you must think about how your actions and beliefs impact others. What do you think about genetics? Pick a topic to focus on: cloning, altering food, genetic testing, mapping out human genes, DNA testing, or another related topic. You can find more topics at *www.kumc.edu/gec*. Research your topic. Then, think about your beliefs surrounding the issue. Write a one-page essay about your reasons for or against this area of genetics—and make sure to back it up with concrete facts from your research.

make tomatoes by using genes from other tomatoes. Looks like a regular tomato, tastes like a regular tomato, and is a regular tomato. But instead of growing in a garden, it was genetically engineered in a lab.

There are many fields geneticists can specialize in. Basic research geneticists are scientists who conduct genetic research on genes. They primarily work in laboratories conducting experiments exploring genes in relation to creating new drugs, foods, and other products.

Medical geneticists are specialized doctors who can diagnose genetic diseases and rare conditions. These are the medical professionals a married couple might consult before deciding to have children if one of the partners has a family history of a genetic disease such as sickle cell anemia, cystic fibrosis, or multiple sclerosis.

According to the National Human Genome Research Institute, genetics counselors are health care professionals with specialized graduate degrees and experience in medical genetics and counseling. Genetic counselors work as members of health care teams providing information and support to individuals or families who have genetic disorders or may be at risk for inherited conditions. Genetic counselors often help by assessing the risk of a genetic disorder by researching a family's history and evaluating medical records, providing counseling and discussing reproductive options.

Education depends largely on the type of genetic career you want. Basic researchers major in genetics or biology as undergraduates. They continue on for their doctorate in genetics and get involved in major research projects. After that, they find work in research institutes, biotechnology companies, or universities. Medical geneticists obtain their medical doctorate with an optional major in biology. Like other physicians, they complete a residency in a specialized area, such as pediatrics, and then focus on a fellowship in clinical genetics. Laboratory geneticists have a minimum bachelor's degree in biology or genetics—but usually a master's degree will open up more career options. Lab training is also a must for these positions. Finally, genetic counselors have their master's degree in genetics, biology, psychology, or social work.

Genetics has drawn lots of attention in recent years with the genome project, cloned sheep, and all the other news-making breakthroughs. There has been a recent increase in the number of people entering the field. There has also been a rise in the number of positions being offered. More and more companies are hiring geneticists in hopes of making new scientific discoveries. And that's good news if you're considering this field.

find your future
home health aide

home health aide

Home health aides provide individualized care to elderly, disabled, and ill people, allowing them to live in the comfort of their own homes instead of in a health facility. By taking care of some of the everyday aspects of care, such as administering oral medications (under physicians' orders or the direction of a nurse) and checking pulse, temperature, and respiration, aides do much of what friends and family would do if they were nearby, trained, and could be with the patient. They might help with simple prescribed exercises or with bathing, dressing, and grooming. They may also change nonsterile dressings, make the patient more comfortable with massages and alcohol rubs, or assist with braces and artificial limbs.

Although we usually think of home health aides in terms of geriatric (elderly) patients, some home health aides specialize in working with teenagers with disabilities or recuperating children. Their jobs might include helping the patient get ready for school or introducing positive activities to help encourage a child who is struggling with the limitations of his or her illness.

Hospice care, provided for patients facing a life-limiting illness or injury, almost always includes home health aides on the patient's team.

Search It!
National Association for Home Care and Hospice at *www.nahc.org* and National Hospice and Palliative Care Organization at *www.nhpco.org*

Read It!
Caring Magazine at *www.caringmagazine.com* and *Spotlight on Caregiving* at *www.caregiving.com*

Learn It!
- High school diploma or general equivalency diploma (GED)
- Training and qualifications vary by state

Earn It!
Average wage is $8.70 per hour. (Source: U.S. Department of Labor)

Find It!
Most home health aides are employed by home health and personal care agencies that assign them to their cases. Find descriptions of job listings at *http://home.health.aide.jobs.monster.com*.

Get Started Now!

- Enroll in health and consumer studies courses in high school.
- Volunteer at a nursing home or long-term care facility.
- Get certified in cardiopulmonary resuscitation (CPR) or basic first aid through your local Red Cross chapter or hospital.
- Take an adult education or community college class to learn the basics of personal health care.

Hire Yourself!

You've passed the certification exam and a home care agency has offered you a position as a home health aide for a reasonably healthy elderly woman. On your first visit to her home, you realize that you are the only person who talks to her each day, and that she looks forward to your visit as much for the social opportunity as for the medical care.

You will be visiting this woman for a long time. Make a list of ways that you can engage her to brighten her day and to help her mind stay sharp. You may want to have a list of topics for conversation (with some lead-in and follow-up questions), a list of things you will bring from home to show her, a list of things you might ask her to show you, and so on. See how many interactions you can plan.

The hospice concept focuses on caring, not curing. It is usually provided in the patient's home, although it can be in a hospice center, nursing home, or other long-term care facility.

Whether elderly, disabled, or facing end-of-life situations, more and more patients and their families are recognizing the benefits of staying in the privacy and comfort of their own homes. The familiarity with surroundings, as well as the sense of security, stability, and independence that a home base can provide, all contribute to a more compassionate approach to dealing with medical issues.

Home health aides have a lot of flexibility in their work. Because many patients need care 24 hours a day, seven days a week, home health aides can often choose among several different work schedules. Some home health aides work with one patient, visiting daily and accommodating any changes in his or her condition. Others work with many different clients, each job lasting a few hours, days, or weeks.

section two

find your future: industrial hygienist

industrial hygienist

As the name suggests, the field of industrial hygiene has its roots in making industrial sites (like factories) more hygienic (translated: cleaner, safer, and better for the workers' health). Some industrial hygienists still do specialize in industrial sites. But today's industrial hygienists also protect people in offices, schools, and other work environments; help communities protect themselves from environmental threats; and recommend and implement responses to environmental accidents and dangers.

Their work is governed by the Occupational Safety and Health Administration (OSHA) and ensures that workplaces are safe for all workers. Their work affects many of us as well, even if we don't work in industrial environments. For instance, you may never see, much less use, a respirator developed to protect factory workers from asbestos or other dangerous byproducts of the manufacturing process. But you will benefit from the furniture, lighting, and computer screen and keyboard designs that result from studies of ways to prevent injuries commonly sustained by office workers.

When industrial hygienists visit workplaces for routine inspections, they may sample the air, soil, or water to check for harmful substances; check on worker scheduling; review processes for dangers or repetitive motions; and check accident histories and compliance with OSHA rules and regulations. Sometimes companies, universities, and other facilities have an internal occupational and environmental health and safety department to conduct this work on their own.

Get Started Now!
- Take lots of math, chemistry, physics, and biology.
- Look for internships or summer jobs with local consultants or with the EPA or OSHA.
- Keep a journal of all the headlines you see that might call for industrial hygienists to become involved.

Search It!
American Industrial Hygiene Association at *www.aiha.org* and National Institute for Occupational Safety and Health at *www.cdc.gov/niosh/about.html*

Read It!
Informational Booklet on Industrial Hygiene found at *www.osha.gov/Publications/OSHA3143/OSHA3143.htm*

Learn It!
- A four-year degree in engineering, chemistry, or biology
- A master's in industrial hygiene for IH technician positions

Earn It!
Median annual salary is $46,186. (Source: U.S. Department of Labor)

Find It!
Government jobs for agencies like the Forest Service, Environmental Protection Agency (EPA), and others are listed at *www.usajobs.opm.gov*.

Hire Yourself!

In addition to their scientific work, industrial hygienists often face the challenge of convincing companies to analyze and make changes to their organization. You've just been hired by the headquarters of a large department store chain to investigate their local stores and evaluate risks to employees and customers. Prepare a presentation that will convince the local branch manager that this is a good idea, including

- the areas of the store you will look at (selling floor, restaurants or snack bars in the store, employee lounge, loading dock, parking lot, restrooms, offices)
- some of the things you may be looking for (safe food handling, safety of escalators and elevators, keeping floors safe in wet weather, good ventilation, peeling paint, fire safety, and so on)
- why finding and correcting any problems could save money as well as the store's reputation

Hint: Look on the Internet for *OSHA* and *retail* or *department stores* for more clues.

Many companies and worksites live in dread of an OSHA inspector appearing at their location (picture your mother making an unannounced white-glove inspection of your room, your backpack, or your school locker). Others have recognized that there is a real advantage to being proactive about calling in the inspectors.

For starters, OSHA consultants are free to the employer. Encouraging voluntary inspections and emphasizing the prevention of injuries and illnesses is more efficient than punishing employers after tragedies occur. Another incentive is that when consultants are called in voluntarily they do not issue citations, report violations, or assign penalties for any violations they might find. They do, however, help employers recognize safety or health hazards, recommend solutions, identify options for obtaining help, and provide safety training for management and employees.

Most situations involving industrial hygienists never come to the attention of the public. But others become part of our everyday life. For instance, an unfortunate transportation accident (a tanker releases millions of gallons of oil into the ocean or a truck or train carrying hazardous materials overturns) that has an immediate impact on wildlife, crops, and people living in the area will undoubtedly be announced on the six o'clock news. In recent years a few high profile cases of families becoming very sick in their own homes have lead to public recognition of the extreme danger of certain types of black mold.

All in all, those with an interest in science, the environment, safety, and helping others may find this an appealing career choice. Experts project average to strong job prospects in this field over the next several years due in part to a continuing public demand for safe work environments and quality products.

Search It!

American Kinesiotherapy Association (AKTA) at **www.akta.org** and American Alliance for Health, Physical Education, Recreation and Dance at **www.aahperd.org**

Read It!

PT Bulletin Online at **www.apta. org/bulletin**, *Sports Science Online* at **www.sportsci.org**, and Kinesiology Net at **www. kinesiology.net**

Learn It!

- Bachelor of science in physical therapy
- Certification through AKTA's Committee on Accreditation of Education Programs for Kinesiotherapy

Earn It!

Median annual salary is $57,330. (Source: U.S. Department of Labor)

Find It!

For information about specific opportunities, go on-line to the Health Promotion Career Network at **www.hpcareer.net**.

kinesiotherapist

If you're looking for a word to summarize what a kinesiotherapist does, the word is movement. But if you're looking for an official definition, turn to the American Physical Therapy Association (APTA). They define kinesiotherapists as health care professionals who, under the direction of a physician, treat the effects of disease, injury, and congenital disorders through the use of therapeutic exercise and education. Simply speaking, kinesiotherapists study the science of human movement and look for ways to improve the efficiency and performance of the human body at work, in sports, and in daily life.

Historically speaking, kinesiotherapy is a fairly new field. According to the American Kinesiotherapy Association, it had its beginnings in World War II and was developed in order to help get troops back into active duty who had survived the war but suffered from illness and injury. Special units with people trained as "corrective therapists" were established to help with rehabilitating soldiers. From there, this type of therapy went on to become a formal training program in medicine. Kinesiology has also broadened its focus to include the prevention of injuries and illnesses in addition to treating them.

Recent years have seen a surge of interest in two particular specialties within kinesiology: sports and the workplace. Sports or exercise kinesio-

Get Started Now!

- Take human anatomy, biology, and psychology courses.
- Learn about various exercises by reading fitness magazines and books.
- Get your first aid certification and keep it current.
- Ask your medical doctor about his or her experience with kinesiotherapists.

Hire Yourself!

Recognizing that you aren't exactly ready to come up with a full-fledged kinesiology treatment plan, we challenge you to add some movement to your life. Use the Internet and resources you find at the library to come up with an exercise regimen consisting of at least five different movement plans (better know as exercises) to help gain the tone, strength, and flexibility that makes for a healthier you.

therapists may be associated with a college or professional sports team, working directly with athletes to develop exercise programs that allow them to move and function better, challenge their cardiovascular strength, or improve their overall fitness. Workplace kinesiotherapists or ergonomic kinesiotherapists specialize in workplace health and safety. They study issues such as posture and repetitive movement and educate workers about techniques they can incorporate in order to avoid common workplace injuries such as carpal tunnel syndrome.

Other main types of kinesiology include biomechanics, which involves treating patients who have chronic diseases or physical disabilities that limit a full range of movement. Pyschomotor kinesiotherapists specialize in working with people diagnosed with problems related to perception, reaction times, and motor learning skills. They typically work with patients who have chronic diseases such as cerebral palsy and autism or with children who are developmentally delayed.

Training to become a kinesiotherapist involves pursuing a college degree that focuses on four primary areas of study: anatomy, biomechanics, physiology, and psychomotor behavior. College training is generally followed by a clinical internship, certification and testing, and perhaps even more schooling in an area such as physical therapy.

If you enjoy helping others and solving problems, this is an excellent career choice. Kinesiotherapists use their professional skills to make people well and their people skills to encourage patients to reach their goals. Patience and the ability to teach others are other key characteristics of kinesiotherapists.

As kinesiology's reputation continues to become recognized as a reliable and viable health care practice, it is expected that increasing numbers of jobs will be available in both private and public health care organizations and in university research centers.

Search It!
American Massage Therapy
Association at ***www.
amtamassage.org***

Read It!
Massage Magazine at ***www.
massagemag.com***, Massage and
Bodywork Resource Center at
www.massageresource.com,
and *BodySense* magazine at
www.bodysensemagazine.com

Learn It!
● Minimum of 500 in-class hours
of state-recognized training
● Accreditation by an organization
such as the Commission on
Massage Training Accreditation
(***www.comta.org***)

Earn It!
Median annual salary is $33,720.
(Source: U.S. Department of Labor)

Find It!
Massage therapists are usually
self-employed and are hired by
chiropractors, health clubs, spas,
and nursing homes.

find your future massage therapist

massage therapist

Ahh! That feels good. If you've ever had a massage, you know the feeling. A good massage therapist uses a healing touch to rub down muscles and make you feel better—physically, mentally, and even emotionally.

Massage therapists don't just prod and poke haphazardly. There's science behind a good back rub. First, massage therapists set a relaxing mood. They may dim lights, play soft music, and heat up a room to a comfortable temperature. They may also light candles and use aromatherapy (a healing technique using essential oils). The idea is to loosen tight muscles and relieve aches and pains through relaxation and therapeutic touch.

Feedback from clients helps guide each 30- to 60-minute session. Massage therapists have to be good at listening—to both verbal comments and nonverbal signs. If a client yelps out in pain, the therapist knows it's a sore spot that needs some tender loving care. If the client dozes off during the massage, the therapist knows he's doing a great job. After all, one of the main objectives is to get the client to relax!

Contrary to popular opinion, massage is not just a "day at the spa" indulgence (although no one disputes that it provides the ultimate way to unwind). More and more physicians are coming to understand and appreciate the benefits of massage. Credible medical evidence points to

Get Started Now!
● Read up on the different types of massage. Large bookstores and libraries will have a plethora of books to choose from.
● Get a massage! Besides feeling better, you'll get a "touching" look at the field.
● Find out if your community's continuing education program offers a beginning massage course and sign up if it does.

Hire Yourself!

Sports, deep tissue, Swedish, Thai, and Shiatsu are popular types of massage. Use Internet and library resources to create a chart comparing the techniques and applications of each type.

massage as a positive means to affect the circulatory, muscular-skeletal, immune, respiratory, and nervous systems. From stress reduction to lowered blood pressure, massage has been proven to help ease various medical conditions. Pain management is another medical use of massage therapy. That's one reason why hospitals, health care facilities, and other medical professionals call on the talents of massage therapists to help patients. Even sports teams hire massage therapists to keep their players' muscles strong and loose.

In the past, anyone with a massage table and a box of candles could claim to be a masseur or masseuse. That's simply not the case today. To be taken seriously as a massage therapist, you need at least 500 hours of formal training from an approved school. After that, you must earn a license to practice in specific states.

Further specialization is also an option, and many therapists choose to go this route. To become specialized in, say, Shiatsu massage or reflexology, therapists have to master the techniques and fully understand the ins and outs of massage.

Massage is a mix of healing art and medical science. According to the American Massage Therapy Association, the best massage therapists bring a balance of academic and technical knowledge, clinical skills, manual dexterity, sensitivity, and awareness to the massage table. The demand for skilled massage therapists is expected to grow as the practice continues to gain acceptance in the medical community and more people experience first-hand the benefits of this healing touch.

Search It!
American Medical Technologists at
www.amt1.com

Read It!
Medical Laboratory Observer at
www.mlo-online.com and AMT
News at ***www.amt1.com/***
amtnews.htm

Learn It!
- Four-year bachelor's degree is required for medical technologists
- Two-year associate's degree is required for medical lab technicians

Earn It!
Median annual salary is $40,186. (Source: U.S. Department of Labor)

Find It!
People in this field work in large hospitals, research labs, pharmaceutical companies, and medical clinics. The Centers for Disease Control and Prevention (***www.cdc.gov***) hires medical technologists, as do other government agencies and public groups.

medical technologist

Have you ever wondered what happens to the blood tests your doctor orders during your annual physical? Do you even want to know what happens to the little cup you fill in the doctor's restroom? In both cases, the specimens end up in a medical laboratory being examined and tested by a medical technologist (MT) or medical lab technician (MLT). Using microscopes along with sophisticated diagnostic tools and procedures, these health care professionals uncover a myriad of information about a person's health. For instance, certain tests are used to diagnose illnesses like diabetes, mononucleosis, or even life-threatening diseases such as AIDS or cancer.

Given that a person's health or even his or her life can depend on accurate test results, it's vital that medical technologists are painstakingly precise and absolutely dependable in their work. This kind of proficiency comes only through training and experience, which is why medical technologists are required to earn a four-year degree in medical laboratory science or a related discipline. Medical lab technicians must complete an associate's degree in medical technology, which includes

Get Started Now!
- Sign up for science courses that require plenty of lab work, which is the essence of this profession.
- Take advanced computer classes to gain a higher level of proficiency with technology.
- Contact your local hospital or diagnostic lab (or ask a teacher or guidance counselor to help) to find a medical technologist in your area. Arrange for an informational interview and a tour of the lab.

Hire Yourself!

Smallpox. Botulism. Salmonella. Even, heaven forbid, the plague. Medical technologists at the Centers for Disease Control and Prevention make it their business to know how to prevent, diagnose, and treat dreaded diseases like these. Click on the Diseases and Conditions icon at *www.cdc.gov* to explore a comprehensive list of biological diseases. Choose one disease to research. Create a poster that illustrates the causes, prevention measures, and diagnostic tests used to keep biological diseases in check.

courses in biological and chemical science as well as math. In addition, both MTs and MLTs must successfully complete a professional certification process through an organization such as an authorized accreditation organization.

According to the American Medical Technologists association, there are six major types of medical laboratory specializations, including

- clinical chemistry—preparing specimens and analyzing the chemical and hormonal contents of body fluids
- microbiology—examining and identifying bacteria and other microorganisms
- blood bank—collecting, typing, and preparing blood and its components for safe transfusion
- immunology—examining responses of the human immune system to foreign bodies such as viruses or allergy-causing agents
- cytotechnology—preparing slides of body cells for microscopic examination of abnormalities that may indicate the presence of cancer
- molecular biology—performing complex genetic testing on cell samples

You can choose one of two paths for a career in this field—medical technologist (bachelor's degree in a lab science, along with a year or more of hands-on clinical training) or medical lab technician (a two-year associate's degree in a lab science). Both options will get you a job in hospitals, laboratories, or health clinics. But the bachelor's degree will open up many more career options, including management work and the choice to specialize.

Search It!
American Society for Microbiology
at **www.asm.org**, the Microbiogy
Network at **www.microbiol.org**,
and Microbe World at
www.microbeworld.org

Read It!
Microbiology Journal at
http://mic.sgmjournals.org and
read the latest news in microbiology at **www.asm.org**

Learn It!
● Bachelor of science degree in
  microbiology
● Most microbiologists go on to
  earn their master's and
  doctorate

Earn It!
Median annual salary is $51,020.
(Source: U.S. Department of Labor)

Find It!
Microbiologists work for large corporations, such as 3M at **www.
mmm.com** or research organizations such as the Center for
Science in the Public Interest at
www.cspinet.org.

find your future
microbiologist

microbiologist

Microbiologists get up close and personal with all types of microorganisms. They become well acquainted with all varieties of microbes, some good microbes (like those found in yogurt) and some bad ones (like those that cause food poisoning).

Generally speaking, microbiologists study living things that are too small to be seen without a microscope (hence the terms *microorganism* and *microbe*). In fact, according to the American Society for Microbiology, microbes are so small and so plentiful that there are more of them on a given person's hand than there are people on the entire planet. They investigate the effects microorganisms have on plants, animals, and humans and determine uses (both positive and negative) microorganisms may have in the environment and people's daily lives.

Needless to say, the microscope is an indispensable tool for this kind of work: if you laid 10,000 microbes in a row, they would only measure about one inch. The work is so precise that sometimes just a single microbe is isolated so that the scientist can analyze it, experiment with it, and do all sorts of tests to see how the microbe reacts to different changes.

Even though they work with the tiniest bits of matter, a microbiologist's job can have huge ramifications. The field of microbiology is so vast that it encompasses several areas of specialization. For instance,

Get Started Now!
● Participate in community, state, and national science fairs.
● Ask a local college or university microbiology department about their ongoing research activities. Discuss
  ways in which you can be involved.
● Get familiar with microbes. Take a look at the photos at
  www.microbeworld.org/htm/aboutmicro/gallery/gallery_start.htm.

Hire Yourself!

What's the difference between bacteria and viruses? Why is it that doctors can prescribe antibiotics to fight many types of bacteria but advise patients to simply tough it out when they come down with a viral infection? Your job is to use Internet and library resources to find out the facts and create a chart that clarifies this mystery once and for all. A good place to start educating yourself is at the American Society of Microbiology student website at *www.microbe. org/microbes/what_is.asp*.

virologists study viruses and how they attack cells, while bacteriologists zone in on how bacteria impact living things. Parasitologists study parasites and how they interact with their hosts.

Depending on their specialty, microbiologists can work in different kinds of settings: labs, hospitals, major companies, universities, and government agencies. In addition to working directly in health-related and pharmaceutical capacities, microbiologists work in a variety of other industries such as food, agriculture, environmental protection, and water treatment.

Becoming a microbiologist requires hefty doses of science courses. Students do best with well-rounded knowledge of biology, chemistry, physics, natural sciences, math, and statistics. While in college, future microbiologists get involved in hands-on lab work. They also work on sharpening their communication skills so that others can understand the inevitable reports and presentations that are part of the job.

Search It!
National Funeral Directors
Association at ***www.nfda.org***

Read It!
"Considering a Career as a
Mortician?" at ***www.***
noevalleyvoice.com/1997/
June/mortu697.html and
American Board of Funeral Service
Education at ***www.abfse.org***

Learn It!
- Two to three years' specialized
  training
- One- to two-year apprenticeship
- Find a list of accredited college
  programs at the American Board
  of Funeral Service Education
  website at ***www.abfse.org***

Earn It!
Median annual salary is $43,380.
(Source: U.S. Department of Labor)

Find It!
The National Funeral Directors
Association website (***www.nfda.***
org) lists job opportunities, as well
as businesses for sale, on their
Professional Resources webpage.

find your mortician future

mortician

Did you have the "ewwww" response when you saw the title of this profile? At least you're still reading—not like those squeamish types who quickly turned the page!

Morticians (or funeral directors) and embalmers (who may be morticians as well) fill a need that has existed in almost every culture throughout history.

Although times and cultures vary greatly, one thing that they all have in common is the need to honor people who die and help their survivors continue to live. And this is where morticians make their contribution.

Most morticians see themselves as being in one of the "helping professions" and take pride in their ability to work with people, helping them with the logistical and emotional aspects of a sad and difficult period in their lives. They also like being in a career that offers such a diverse array of responsibilities.

Morticians must be knowledgeable about the relevant laws, including the conditions that require embalming (no, it is not always necessary), the requirements to permit cremation (in some states, all surviving children must agree in writing) or donation of the body for research or education, and requirements for transport of bodies (many people want to be buried in their hometown, rather than the place to which they have moved). Morticians need to know all about filing for a death certificate and claiming life insurance payments, as well as benefits available from

Get Started Now!
- Take lots of science classes: most mortuary science programs include microbiology, pathology, chemistry, and anatomy.
- Volunteer at a funeral home. You may just be washing cars and replenishing tissue boxes, but you'll be in a good position to watch and learn.

Hire Yourself!

You are ready to begin your apprenticeship as a funeral director. You will be working in a suburban area just outside of a large city with a very diverse population. Your new boss has strongly suggested that you become familiar with some of the major religions represented in the area.

Create a grid that will help you compare the similarities and differences among the following three religious groups: Christians, Jews, and Muslims. Issues you'll want to investigate include the traditions and taboos related to preparing the body for burial, funeral timeline, and customary elements of the funeral service.

Use a favorite Internet search engine such as Google or Yahoo and use search terms such as *Jewish AND funerals* to find information about each of the faiths.

Social Security and from the Veterans Administration, and how to help families receive those benefits.

Morticians need to have some knowledge of many different cultural and religious customs and traditions. They cannot risk offending a family by offering a service that is strictly forbidden by that family's religious or ethnic group.

Many morticians own their own funeral homes. As business owners, they need to know about accounting, hiring and managing employees, setting prices and billing customers, advertising and marketing, local tax laws, record-keeping, and business registration requirements.

Some morticians have compared themselves to butlers who run large estates. They need to be organized and efficient and familiar with resources in their community and around the country to provide for all the needs of the client. It is usually the mortician, not the family, who makes the arrangements with the cemetery, provides transportation for the remains and the family, arranges for clergy or other officiators, and even places notices in the local newspapers.

Morticians may also be licensed as embalmers or may hire and supervise embalmers. Embalming has been around since the old, old days of ancient Egypt. Today, embalmers wash, preserve, and apply make-up to the deceased. In some cases, they work with clay, wax, or other materials to shape and restore body parts.

Embalmers should be in good health and not allergic to the chemicals used in the process. They should have reasonable physical strength for required lifting.

Morticians and funeral directors need to dress conservatively and appropriately. They should have courtesy, tact, understanding, emotional stability, and the ability to communicate easily with individuals and groups of people. Career success depends on a calm, patient attitude, self-control, tact, flexibility, and a good memory for names and faces. As one mortician pointed out, "Can't remember who's who? Don't become a funeral director. You never, ever, want to say how sorry you are about somebody's mother and then find out it's their aunt!"

nuclear medicine technician

nuclear medicine technician At first glance, the idea of using radioactive substances to heal someone may seem a little strange. But that's exactly what nuclear medicine technologists (NMTs) do every day. They use very small (and thus, safe) doses of radioactive materials to conduct more than a hundred different kinds of diagnostic tests and therapeutic treatments. These procedures are so precise that there isn't a single major human organ that cannot be targeted.

Bottom line: through nuclear medicine, doctors now have access to information that they've never had access to before without actually performing surgery. This allows them to identify problems earlier, which, in turn, means that they are able to treat diseases in earlier stages when the chance of recovery is greatest. The procedures themselves are safe, painless, and relatively inexpensive.

When nuclear medicine is used for diagnostic purposes, very small amounts of radioactive materials (called radioisotopes or tracers) are introduced into the patient's body by mouth, by injection, or some other means. The tracers are carefully directed toward specific organs, bones, or tissues, and they provide emissions that reveal essential information about

Search It!
Society of Nuclear Medicine at **www.snm.org** and American Society of Radiologic Technologists at **www.asrt.org**

Read It!
The *Journal of Nuclear Medicine* offers a variety of articles at **www.snm.org**

Learn It!
- One- to four-year degree from an accredited nuclear medicine technology program
- Accredited nuclear medicine technology programs are listed at **www.jrcnmt.org**

Earn It!
Median annual salary for nuclear medicine technicians is $48,750. (Source: U.S. Department of Labor)

Find It!
Nuclear medicine technicians work for medical labs, biotechnology firms, and large pharmaceutical corporations. Major employers include Pfizer at **www.pfizer.com** and GlaxoSmithKline at **www.gsk.com/careers/joinus.htm**.

Get Started Now!
- Load up on courses in chemistry, biology, anatomy, and mathematics.
- Call your local hospital and ask to set up a visit with the nuclear medicine technician.
- Find all kinds of nuclear medical resources by clicking the *Resources for . . . Technologist Students* icon at **http://interactive.snm.org**.

Hire Yourself!

Get inside your organs! Pick an organ, any organ. Use the Internet or medical encyclopedias to gather illustrations, photos, and information about the organ. Get out your colored pencils and make a scientific drawing of it. Make sure to label major parts of the organ and use a color-coded key to identify minor parts. Write up a one-paragraph description of the organ and paste it on the back of your drawing. This project makes for a handy reference—and very cool piece of artwork!

certain diseases or types of cancers. An especially unique aspect of nuclear medicine is that this technique actually documents body function. Other kinds of tests such as X rays simply reveal an organ's structure.

The medical community continues to make great strides in treating diseases with radioisotopes. Currently they are used successfully for treatment of diseases such as thyroid and prostrate cancer and hyperthyroidism. In addition, the Federal Drug Administration (FDA) is approving new therapies at a very promising rate. Some researchers predict that before long more than 80% of cancer types will be treatable with nuclear medicine.

Nuclear medicine technicians work directly with patients in administering tests and treatments. Other types of nuclear medicine professionals include nuclear physicians, who are generally involved in research and the formulation of patient diagnosis and treatments. According to the Society of Nuclear Medicine, nuclear pharmacists focus on procuring, compounding, quality control testing, dispensing, distributing, and monitoring of the radiopharmaceuticals used in nuclear medicine.

Although the small amounts of radioactive material used in nuclear tests and treatments are virtually identical to the amount used in regular X rays, people who work with the materials on a daily basis are required to take certain precautions. For instance, protective clothing such as gloves and special shields are routinely used, as are shielded syringes.

The future is bright for this career—and that's not the radiation talking. According to the Society of Nuclear Medicine, there are 14,000 nuclear medicine technicians in the United States. As more uses are found for nuclear therapy, especially in the fight against cancer, more opportunities will become available.

find your nurse future

nurse

Where's a good nurse when you need one? Apparently, qualified nurses are hard to find in certain parts of the country. So hard to find, in fact, that some experts are projecting a shortage of up to 434,000 nurses by the year 2020. The shortage is so acute that a national recruitment effort is underway, led in part by Johnson & Johnson (see their website at **www.discovernursing.com**), to encourage people to consider nursing as a career path. This is good news for job seekers with an interest in helping, healing, and taking care of others.

Becoming a nurse involves making several choices. First is a choice about training. It takes one year of specialized training to become a licensed practical nurse (LPN). LPNs handle basic patient care tasks such as taking vital signs, giving injections, and administering routine bedside care. It takes two to four years of college training to become a registered nurse (RN). RNs are entrusted with higher levels of responsibility and provide direct patient care, assist physicians during examinations and treatments, develop and manage nursing care plans, and instruct patients and their family in proper care techniques.

Beyond the training, nurses have a variety of choices about where they work. Many nurses opt to work in hospitals, while others work in doctor's offices, assisted living facilities, medical clinics, schools, government health departments, large corporations and factories, and laboratories. Increasing numbers of nurses find employment as home health

Search It!
American Nurses Association at **www.nursingworld.org** and National League of Nursing at **www.nln.org**

Read It!
Online Journal of Issues in Nursing at **http://nursingworld.org/ojin** and Discover Nursing at **www.discovernursing.com**

Learn It!
- One year of nurse's training is required to become a licensed practical nurse (LPN)
- Completion of a two-year associate's degree or four-year bachelor's degree in nursing is required to become a registered nurse (RN)
- State license in nursing

Earn It!
Median annual salary for registered nurses is $48,090.
(Source: U.S. Department of Labor)

Find It!
To get a better idea of the kind of opportunities available, go on-line to **www.nursingspectrum.com**.

Get Started Now!
- Take high school classes in science (especially biology and chemistry), psychology, and health.
- Get certified in cardiopulmonary resuscitation (CPR) and first aid through your local hospital or Red Cross chapter.
- Volunteer at a hospital or offer to help out in your school nurse's office.

Hire Yourself!

Nursing is definitely not a one-size-fits-all kind of profession. There's a different "size" for every interest. Find out the diverse array of nursing options at websites such as *www.discovernursing.com/specialties.asp* and *www. nursingsociety.org/career/nursing_orgs.html*.

Pick one specialty that sounds especially interesting to you and use the information you find to write a recruitment brochure to encourage young people to consider this particular career path in nursing.

aide nurses, checking in on patients who are chronically ill or recuperating from an injury or illness in the comfort of their home.

Besides workplace options, nurses often choose to specialize in certain types of nursing. In hospitals, nursing specialties range from critical care and oncology to surgery and maternity, among others. Nurses may choose to work with the very youngest of patients in neonatal care units or pediatricians' offices or they may choose the oldest of patients in gerontological care settings. There are also forensics nurses who work specifically with victims of abuse, violence, criminal activity, or traumatic accidents. Public health nurses fulfill research and public education roles in various types of government and private agencies. In addition, all branches of the military provide interesting opportunities for nurses that often include good training and scholarship benefits as well as assignments in places all over the world.

A typical day for a nurse largely depends on where he or she works. Hospital nurses usually work in a specific area. So a maternity nurse, for example, may help deliver several babies a day. A nurse assigned to surgery will help prep a patient and make sure paperwork is taken care of before wheeling him to the operating room. Nurses who work in nursing homes assist and care for the elderly, while public health nurses deal with a variety of people and problems every day.

Flexibility is one of the benefits of nursing. Depending on a nurse's availability and interests, she or he may choose to work a traditional nine-to-five schedule or may seek out any number of part-time or rotating shift schedules. Most nurses will tell you that one of the best parts of the job is knowing that their work really makes a difference in the lives of others.

Opportunity is knocking for people with an interest in nursing as a profession. Training, scholarships, and even signing bonuses are common incentives in some areas.

find your future
occupational therapist

Search It!
American Occupational Therapy Association at *www.aota.org*

Read It!
American Journal of Occupational Therapy at *www.aota.org/ajot/index.asp*

Learn It!
- Bachelor's degree in occupational therapy
- Six months of supervised fieldwork and successful completion of the national certification examination
- Master's degree improves salary and employment options

Earn It!
Median annual salary is $51,090. (Source: US Department of Labor)

Find It!
Many occupational therapists have their own practices, while others work for schools, hospitals, and health institutions. To get a better idea of available opportunities, go on-line to *http://aota.jobcontrolcenter.com/search.cfm*.

occupational therapist

Picture this: a child who had his legs amputated wins first place in a running race. And, not only that, he gets to the finish line in record-breaking time. With the help of prosthetic legs, he was able to realize his athletic dream. Chances are an occupational therapist (OT) was with him every step of the way.

Occupational therapists work with patients to help with physical and mental health disabilities. Many of the patients that OTs work with have severe injuries that seriously impair the person's capabilities. The therapist's job is to help the patient adjust to the handicap and to make life more enjoyable and productive.

The term *occupational* in this career title can be confusing. To these therapists, *occupation* is not just what one does for employment. It includes everything that we do, from leisure activities to taking care of ourselves. The goal of an occupational therapist is to help clients improve their strength and dexterity, to help them regain physical or mental ability to perform the basic tasks of life, and to compensate for permanent disabilities. They also recommend or help to design special

Get Started Now!
- Volunteer at a rehab center, camp, or other activity program for physically- or mentally-challenged children.
- Keep your grades up! Getting into occupational therapy programs is competitive.
- Read profiles of Paralympic athletes (*www.paralympic.org*) and watch the games to see how OTs helped with training.

Hire Yourself!

Occupational therapy often involves using a variety of tools that enable patients to function at optimum levels. Go on-line to look through some of the products offered by companies such as *www.isokineticsinc.com/facility.htm* and *www.promedproducts.com*. Pick 10 tools that you think would be essential for a new occupational therapist to have. Print out pictures and descriptions and compile a mini-catalog featuring these "must-have" items. Be sure to include your comments and recommendations regarding each tool.

equipment that will enable clients to better communicate or interact with their environments.

Occupational therapists work with children who have birth defects or injuries from accidents and with older people who have had strokes or heart attacks. They often work in hospitals and long-term care institutions with a number of patients, each of whom may have different capabilities. Occupational therapists works to plan programs and activities that help all patients in the group work their minds and their bodies. Activities can range from daily exercise classes to art and music, and everything in between.

Occupational therapists have to get creative. They learn to see everyday objects in a different light. For example, if a patient without fingers wants to paint, the OT can track down or even create a paintbrush that's designed for the mouth or the feet. Coming up with new ways to solve problems is all in a day's work.

Getting others to complete a difficult task is one of the challenges of this career. Occupational therapists need to possess three Ps: persistence, patience, and praise. Persistence is crucial, as is convincing patients to be persistent, because giving up is easier than working your hardest for an end result. So OTs have to be patient with their patients. People learn at their own pace, and when an illness or injury is involved, that pace can be slower than average. That's where praise comes in. OTs encourage and praise their clients during treatment and cheer them on to success.

In-depth knowledge of behavior, personality, injury, and disease is necessary. OTs gain these smarts while majoring in occupational therapy in college. Upon graduating, they must complete an internship at a licensed facility and pass a certification exam.

find your optometrist future

Search It!
Future Optometrists at
www.futureoptometrist.com,
National Optometric Association at
www.natoptassoc.org, and
American Optometric Association
at **www.aoanet.org**

optometrist

Do you wear glasses or contact lenses? If so, you're part of a very large group that includes more than half of the people in the United States. And if you are part of that group, you have probably had experience with an optometrist, or Doctor of Optometry.

Optometrists use specialized equipment to identify vision problems, eye injuries, and eye conditions like glaucoma, cataracts, and retinal disorders. They prescribe glasses and contact lenses to correct vision problems, as well as medications to treat specific problems, and refer problems requiring surgery to ophthalmologists. In many states, optometrists are also permitted to perform laser assisted in situ keratomileusis (LASIK) surgery, to provide patients with good eyesight without the need for corrective lenses.

Optometrists are often confused with ophthalmologists, physicians who perform eye surgery for cataracts and other serious problems. Ophthalmologists, like optometrists, also examine eyes and prescribe eyeglasses and contact lenses. Opticians, other eye professionals sometimes confused with optometrists, can fit and adjust glasses (and contact lenses in some states) according to prescriptions written by ophthalmologists or optometrists. They cannot examine patients or write prescriptions themselves.

Most optometrists are generalists—they work with anyone who comes into their shop or office. Their patients typically suffer from blurry vision, caused by nearsightedness (myopia), farsightedness (hyperopia), or astig-

Read It!
Read about vision therapy, visual training, and visual perception at
www.vision3d.com

Learn It!
● A bachelor's degree geared for science majors or health professionals
● Complete a doctorate program in optometry from an accredited four-year program

Earn It!
Median annual salary is $86,090.
(Source: U.S. Department of Labor)

Find It!
Many optometrists own their own private practice. Others work for department stores, small local stores, or for large chains such as LensCrafters.

Get Started Now!

● Get your own eyes checked. Ask your optometrist about testing for vision problems other than distance viewing.
● Load up on anatomy, biology, physics, and math courses through high school and college.

Hire Yourself!

You've been an optometrist for a retail store in the local shopping mall for the past three years. Now you want to open your own business. Write a plan for your optometry business that includes the following: what you will specialize in, if anything; the name of your shop; what type of location you will look for (in business, shopping, or residential neighborhood); where you will advertise; what will be different about your shop to make people want to go to it.

matism. Their older patients often suffer from presbyopia, the inability to change focus from far to near ("reading glasses syndrome").

Other optometrists choose to work as vision researchers or to specialize in one of these areas:

- Developmental or behavioral optometry: These optometrists look for problems with visual skills that are related to learning. These skills include visual tracking (which shows up as losing one's place when reading, or constantly rereading a line), eye coordination, eye teaming (binocular vision), eye movement, color vision, and other visual perceptual skills. You can learn more about what these optometrists do at the Parents Active for Vision Education (PAVE) website at *www.pavevision.org/behavioraloptometrist.htm*.
- Sports vision: Often people with 20/20 vision can improve their athletic performance by improving eye motion, depth perception, or wearing tinted lenses that improve color contrast. For more information, check out the Connecticut Association of Optometrists (*www.cao.org/sports.htm*).
- Low vision services: Low vision specialists help visually impaired patients.
- Occupational vision: These optometrists work with businesses to protect and preserve workers' vision and minimize eyestrain.
- Geriatric or pediatric optometry: These specialists diagnose and treat problems common to older patients or to children.

The job market for optometrists is strong. There are only 17 colleges of optometry in the United States and Puerto Rico, so admission is very competitive. You need to have a strong math and science background and do well on the optometry admissions test.

find your pharmacist future

pharmacist

The common image of a pharmacist is that of someone dispensing medications and giving information about prescription and over-the-counter medications. These retail pharmacists also instruct patients on how to properly take a drug, tell them about the drug's possible side effects, and watch for possible interactions with other medications the patient may be taking.

Retail pharmacy is just one of many different specializations in this field. Others include nuclear pharmacists who mix radioactive drugs that may be used as medications or for testing procedures such as computed tomography (CT) and positron emission tomography (PET) scans. Because these drugs have a very short life span once mixed, nuclear pharmacists often work at night in order to fill prescriptions needed for the following day.

Clinical pharmacists are another specialty. They work as part of the patient's health care team, providing drug information to the physician staff at a hospital. Clinical pharmacists monitor drug therapies and make recommendations to physicians about medications, dosage, and duration of therapy. They may also supervise the compounding and dispensing of drugs and intravenous solutions and oversee quality assurance functions.

Hospital pharmacists are responsible for dispensing medications and advising patients on how to use prescribed medications at home. The

Get Started Now!

- Beef up your schedule with science and math courses (especially biology and chemistry).
- Inquire about summer job opportunities at local community drugstores.
- Talk to local pharmacists about their work.
- Learn about the tools once used by pharmacists at **www.collectmedicalantiques.com/apothecary.html**.

Search It!
American Association of Colleges of Pharmacy at **www.aacp.org** and American Association of Pharmaceutical Scientists at **www.aaps.org**

Read It!
Pharmacy Times at **www. pharmacytimes.com**, *U.S. Pharmacist* at **www. uspharmacist.com**

Learn It!
Pharmacy licensing currently requires a PharmD or Doctor of Pharmacy degree, an internship, and passing a state licensing exam.

Earn It!
Median annual salary is $77,050. (Source: U.S. Department of Labor)

Find It!
Many jobs are listed at websites such as Pharmacy Now (**www. pharmacynow.com**) and Rx Career Center (**www. pharmacyjobs.rxcareercenter. com**).

Hire Yourself!

Select a serious illness (like HIV/AIDS, cancer, or schizophrenia) and see what drugs are currently being developed as potential cures for that illness. Look for drugs currently being tested at *www.centerwatch.com* or *www.clinicaltrials.gov*. Check the research or news section of websites from some of the larger pharmaceutical companies such as Hoffman LaRoche, Pfizer, Bristol-Myers Squibb, Merck, or Novartis. Write a one-page opinion paper on a drug that you think sounds particularly promising.

hospital pharmacist may also monitor inventory and order supplies and medications, fill IVs, and mix chemotherapy compounds.

Other areas recognized by the Board of Pharmaceutical Specialties include nutrition support pharmacist, oncology (cancer) pharmacist, and psychiatric pharmacist.

Some pharmacists work for pharmaceutical companies, helping to develop new medicines, answering questions about existing ones, or even acting as sales representatives who educate doctors about new products. Other pharmacists work for health plans or insurance companies, setting up drug benefit programs, recommending the drugs that should be covered, and being the on-call pharmacist to help doctors and patients with questions about various drugs or drug interactions.

Pharmacologists do not work directly with patients or doctors. They are part of the scientific research team that develops and tests new medications. Their work includes designing experiments, devising and testing hypotheses, and analyzing and interpreting data. Research and report writing are large parts of their job—they have to study reports of what was tried before and come up with ways to do better.

In the past, a bachelor of science degree in chemistry was mandatory for entry into pharmacy school. The new requirements shave off two years of undergraduate work. The four-year Doctor of Pharmacy program requires only two years of prior college study in prepharmacy education. Prerequisite courses include mathematics, chemistry, biology, and physics. After pharmaceutical school, pharmacists may choose fellowships or residencies in specialized programs. Pharmacists who plan to own their own pharmacy may also obtain a master's degree in business administration.

phlebotomist

Phlebotomists are the health care professionals who collect blood specimens or blood donations. Blood specimens are sent to a medical laboratory for any number of diagnostic tests, while blood donations are put through a rigorous screening and preparation process.

At a minimum, phlebotomists must be high school graduates who participated in a specialized training program at a technical school or community college and perhaps received some on-the-job lab experience. However, it's quite common for health care facilities to sponsor other medical technicians or assistants to become phlebotomists to increase their skills and usefulness in serving patients. In most states, phlebotomists must be certified, although requirements vary by state.

As for the types of skills and traits most needed by phlebotomists, a calm personality and steady hand are givens. The professionals know that drawing blood is no big deal, but sometimes they have to be able to alleviate the fears of needle-phobic patients.

The ability to get blood quickly and comfortably would most certainly be near the top of the skill list written from the patient's perspective. Blood samples may be drawn by skin puncture (the finger prick that you've probably experienced at one time or another), by venipuncture (from a vein), or by arterial collection (from an artery).

The blood vessels that you see close to the surface of your own body are veins. A good phlebotomist can judge a vein's color, width, and

Get Started Now!
- Take classes in biology and health sciences.
- Learn as much medical terminology as you can. Good resources include medical handbooks, medical dictionaries, and the Internet.

Search It!
American Society of Phlebotomy Technicians at **www.aspt.org**

Read It!
"The Facts" at **www. myblooddraw.com** and Hemapheresis ONline at **www. pheresis.org/journals.html**

Learn It!
- High school diploma or GED
- Certification in phlebotomy, generally requiring four weeks to six months of specialized training, plus six hours of continuing education each year

Earn It!
Median annual salary is $21,944. (Source: U.S. Department of Labor)

Find It!
Phlebotomists work in hospitals, health clinics, blood donation centers, and laboratories. Go on-line to **www.bloodcenterjobs.com** to find out about opportunities in the profession.

Hire Yourself!

Create a chart showing some of the reasons doctors order blood tests. Include columns for: Reason for Test, Type of Test (artery, vein, or skin), and whether the test is for Initial Diagnosis or Ongoing Monitoring. Enter the keywords *blood test*, possibly with *vein* or *artery*, into your favorite Internet search engine. Or search for *blood test* at medical information sites like Medline Plus (U.S. National Library of Medicine) at *www.medlineplus.gov*; *www.DrKoop.com*; and the "About Blood" section at *www.aabb.org*.

how close it is to the surface of the skin and get a quick and painless sample. Arteries are deeper, or further from the surface of your skin, and harder to reach. Blood taken from veins is very different from blood taken from arteries. Arteries take blood away from the heart. Arterial blood gives information about how much oxygen or other blood gases your blood is carrying. Veins take blood back to the heart. That blood has collected viruses and other materials from the organs it has passed through.

Technical ability to perform diagnostic procedures accurately and efficiently is key. With people's health and even, in some cases, their lives at stake, there is no room for mistakes. Doctors and clinicians must be able to count on accurate results in order to correctly diagnose and treat a wide variety of diseases. In today's high-tech environment, this means that phlebotomists have to be comfortable using computers and other equipment for the analysis.

Experts are optimistic about the future of this medical specialty, not only because of a growing and aging population, but also because of exciting new developments in blood tests themselves. Researchers are currently hard at work looking at ways to predict certain conditions, such as heart attacks, before they occur. The promising results indicate the potential of a whole new frontier for phlebotomy as a preventive strategy.

find your future physical therapist

physical therapist

What do a construction worker with an injured back, an elderly person with arthritis, a pregnant woman, and a disabled child have in common? They all have good reasons to see a physical therapist. Physical therapists work to improve the strength and mobility of patients with injuries, disease, or disabilities. They also use their skills to help relieve pain due to chronic illness or injury and to prevent or limit physical disabilities.

Common reasons to see a physical therapist include low back pain, carpal tunnel syndrome, stroke rehabilitation, cardiac rehabilitation, and chronic respiratory problems. Physical therapists work with patients in every stage of the human lifespan—from the very youngest babies to the very oldest adults.

Typical types of physical treatments include therapeutic exercise training. In certain cases, physical therapists administer treatment using special equipment like moist packs, ultraviolet and infrared lamps, and ultrasound machines. At times they may use special traction equipment or deep tissue massage to relieve pain in specific muscles or joints.

A big part of the job entails educating patients on treatment plans and procedures, demonstrating proper techniques, and encouraging consistent and accurate forms of exercise and activity that patients can practice on their own. Physical therapists also devote part of their time to preparing treatment plans and reports.

Search It!
American Physical Therapy Association at **www.apta.org**

Read It!
PT Magazine at **www.apta. org/ptmagazine** and Physical Therapy: The Web Space at **www.automailer.com/tws**

Learn It!
● Bachelor of science degree in physical therapy
● Master's degree may be required for advancement

Earn It!
Median annual salary is $57,330. (Source: U.S. Department of Labor)

Find It!
Physical therapists work in hospitals, health clinics, health care facilities, and rehabilitation centers. You can seek out specific kinds of opportunities in specific geographic locations at **www. apta.org/bulletin/job_listings**.

Get Started Now!
● Take several science classes, including anatomy, biology, physics, and physiology.
● Volunteer to help your school's athletic trainer. Her work shares certain aspects with physical therapy such as working to rehabilitate injured athletes and implementing doctor-ordered treatment plans.

Hire Yourself!

Go on-line to the Physical Therapy Web Space at *http://doree.com/tws/disease.html*. Here you'll find a list of ailments frequently requiring physical therapy treatments along with links to information directly related to each ailment. Choose one disease and seek out three kinds of information: a definition of the disease itself, a list of the disease's primary symptoms, and a description of common physical therapy treatments used to alleviate the symptoms. Record this information in a fact sheet suitable for use in educating patients about this condition.

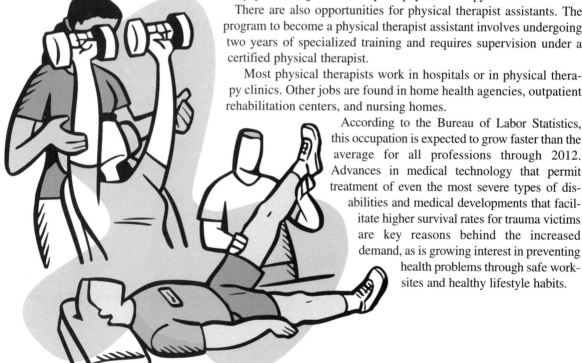

All physical therapists are college graduates and all are required to pass a national exam and be licensed in the state where they practice. It's not uncommon for physical therapists to pursue a master's degree or advanced certification in an area of specialization such as cardiopulmonary, pediatric, geriatric, or sports physical therapy.

There are also opportunities for physical therapist assistants. The program to become a physical therapist assistant involves undergoing two years of specialized training and requires supervision under a certified physical therapist.

Most physical therapists work in hospitals or in physical therapy clinics. Other jobs are found in home health agencies, outpatient rehabilitation centers, and nursing homes.

According to the Bureau of Labor Statistics, this occupation is expected to grow faster than the average for all professions through 2012. Advances in medical technology that permit treatment of even the most severe types of disabilities and medical developments that facilitate higher survival rates for trauma victims are key reasons behind the increased demand, as is growing interest in preventing health problems through safe worksites and healthy lifestyle habits.

find your physician future

physician

Nothing explains the role of a physician better than Medicine's Social Contract with Humanity, a pledge made by delegates of the American Medical Association in the aftermath of September 11, 2001. Through this common document, physicians committed themselves to the fulfillment of nine tasks:

- Respect human life and the dignity of every individual.
- Refrain from supporting or committing crimes against humanity and condemn all such acts.
- Treat the sick and injured with competence and compassion and without prejudice.
- Apply our knowledge and skills when needed, though doing so may put us at risk.
- Protect the privacy and confidentiality of those for whom we care and breach that confidence only when keeping it would seriously threaten their health and safety or that of others.
- Work freely with colleagues to discover, develop, and promote advances in medicine and public health that ameliorate suffering and contribute to human well-being.
- Educate the public and polity about present and future threats to the health of humanity.
- Advocate for social, economic, educational, and political changes that ameliorate suffering and contribute to human well-being.

Get Started Now!

- Take college prep courses with heavy concentrations in math and science.
- Volunteer at a local hospital or public health clinic to get a firsthand look at the profession.
- Find out about job-shadowing and tour opportunities at your local hospital.

Search It!
American Medical Association at **www.ama-assn.org** and American Osteopathic Association at **www.osteopathic.org**

Read It!
New England Journal of Medicine at **http://content.nejm.org** and *American Medical News* at **www. ama-assn.org/amednews**

Learn It!
- Completion of four-year premedical undergraduate degree
- Four years of medical school followed by three to eight years of internship and residency (depending on chosen area of specialization)

Earn It!
Salary varies by speciality from $150,267 to $306,964. (Source: U.S. Department of Labor)

Find It!
To find postings of currently available positions for physicians, go to **www.nejmjobs.org**.

Hire Yourself!

Go on-line to MedBioWorld at *www.medbioworld.com* where you'll find links to 35,000 medical journals, associations, and databases. Choose a specialty that interests you and follow the link to find out pertinent information that includes a complete description of the specialty and the types of medical problems it covers and specific facts about training and residency requirements. Prepare a well-organized fact sheet using your findings.

• Teach and mentor those who follow us for they are the future of our caring profession.

This may seem like a tall order to fill, but it certainly helps explain why medicine is one of the most respected and highly paid professions. Saving lives is just part of a day's work for many physicians. They diagnose illnesses, prescribe medications, examine patients, and order, perform, and interpret diagnostic tests. They are advocates for preventive health care and provide life-saving counsel on sensitive areas such as smoking, sexually transmitted diseases, and even safe driving.

Preparing to become a physician can be a daunting process requiring years of education. The educational process begins with completion of a premed bachelor's degree (four years). Then there are four years of medical school followed by a three- to six-year residency (depending on the area of specialization). Entry into medical school is so competitive that this profession tends to attract the "cream of the crop." Those students with the highest grade point averages (GPAs) and most impressive extracurricular credentials have the best chance of admission.

There are a wide variety of specializations available to physicians, most of which fall into three main categories: primary care, medical specialties, and surgical specialties. Primary care doctors include general and family practitioners, pediatricians, and internists. Medical care specialties include allergists, dermatologists, obstetricians, pathologists, psychiatrists, and cardiologists, among others. Surgeons may choose to specialize in areas such as general surgery, neurological surgery, ophthalmology, pulmonology, and orthopedic surgery.

Experts project continued demand for physicians in the coming years. Demand is expected to be heaviest in specialties that serve older adults and those that focus on preventive care. They also predict that the current trend of most physicians setting up their own private practices will shift toward working as employees in group medical practices and integrated health care facilities.

Search It!

American Association of Physician Assistants (AAPA) at *www.aapa.org* and National Commission on Certification of Physician Assistants at *www.nccpa.net*

Read It!

P.A. Forum—The P.A. Resource Center at *www.physicianassociate.com* and Student Academy of the American Academy of Physician Assistants at *www.saaapa.aapa.org*

Learn It!

- Bachelor's degree (or a minimum of two years of college and some health care experience)
- Specialized physician assistant training program (usually at least 26 months)

Earn It!

Median annual salary is $64,670. (Source: U.S. Department of Labor)

Find It!

To find information about current positions, go on-line to *www.physicianassistantjobs.com*.

find your future
physician assistant

physician assistant

If you love the medical field, enjoy the challenge of diagnosing and treating medical problems, and have a real knack for working with people, you may have considered becoming a doctor. But then again you may have become so overwhelmed by the number of years of study, internship, and residency required (and the accompanying mountain of student loan debt) that you might have nixed the idea of working as a physician. If that's the case, opting for a P.A. after your name instead of M.D. may prove to be the next best choice for you.

Physician assistants (or PAs) do almost everything that physicians do. Their license permits them to perform physical exams, diagnose illnesses, order and interpret lab tests and X rays, counsel patients, and order or carry out different types of therapy. Physician assistants are able to write prescriptions in almost every state and can even work as first or second assistants during major surgery

On the administrative side, physician assistants may manage areas of a health care facility, order medical and laboratory supplies, supervise technicians and assistants, and mentor new PAs. They may meet with pharmaceutical sales reps to learn more about new drugs and get sam-

Get Started Now!

- Emphasize college prep courses in your high school schedule.
- Volunteer at a hospital, medical office, or health clinic. Even if you're not working directly with patients, you are still getting a good feel for what these professionals' days are really like.

Hire Yourself!

You're a physician assistant in a well-known cancer treatment center. The patient to whom you've been assigned doesn't want to talk to you—he only wants a "real doctor." Make a list of the things you can say to him to assure him that you will provide excellent care. Then try role-playing the situation with a friend or relative to see how convincing you can be. Remember that your statements can include tangibles (like technical training and experience) and intangibles (like bedside manner and workload).

ples for their patients. They are also responsible for keeping their patients' medical records up to date.

One limitation that PAs do have is that they must work under the supervision of a licensed physician. However, even that requirement has some flexibility in daily practice. Because PAs are often used where there are shortages of doctors (such as rural areas or inner-city clinics), their actual contact with their supervising physician may be somewhat limited.

About half of all PAs work in primary care areas, such as general internal medicine, pediatrics, and family medicine. About 20 percent work in surgery and related fields, and the others specialize in everything from dermatology to emergency medicine, orthopedics, or geriatrics. Most PAs work in a doctor or dentist's office or clinic, with hospitals being the next most common job setting. Others work in public health clinics, prisons, schools, and home health care agencies.

There is a lot of competition among people applying to PA programs. Many of the applicants are nurses, paramedics, or emergency medical technicians (EMTs) who want to further their careers. In general, to be accepted to a PA training program, you need strong college grades (some programs look for as high as a 3.5 grade point average), a strong background in science classes, and at least one year of related experience.

Because PAs work so closely with doctors, their training is very similar. The first phase is classroom work, with an emphasis on biochemistry, anatomy, microbiology, disease prevention, clinical pharma- cology, and medical ethics. The second phase is a series of clinical rotations through different areas of medicine. After completing the required coursework, graduates still have to pass a national certification exam. Throughout their career, PAs are required to take ongoing medical education classes (at least 100 hours of classroom time every two years) and must retake the certification test every six years to maintain their national certification.

Search It!
American Veterinary Medical Association at ***www.avma.org*** and National Association of Veterinary Technicians in America at ***www.navta.net***

Read It!
Find links to the *American Journal of Veterinary Research* at ***www. avma.org/publications/ default.asp***

Learn It!
- Undergraduate degree in biological or physiological sciences
- Four years of specialized training at an accredited veterinary school. For a list of approved schools see Association of American Veterinary Medical Colleges at ***http://aavmc.org***

Earn It!
Median annual salary is $63,090. (Source: U.S. Department of Labor)

Find It!
For listings of current vet jobs, see ***www.avma.org/vcc/default.asp***.

find **veterinarian** your future

veterinarian

A veterinarian is to animals what a physician is to people. When animals get sick or are injured, veterinarians follow similar procedures to diagnose and treat their furry or feathery patients. Just like a physician, a veterinarian's primary duties fall into two categories: keeping animals healthy and helping sick animals get better.

Preventive measures include conducting annual physical exams, giving shots, and running tests. Treating sick or injured animals includes troubleshooting problems, prescribing medications, treating injuries, and, in some cases, may even involve performing surgeries. Surgical procedures run the gamut from sterilization surgeries (neutering for males, spaying for females) to performing emergency surgery on an animal that has been hit by a car.

Most veterinarians specialize in small, domesticated animals—house pets such as dogs, cats, and the like. These vets typically work in specially equipped offices or animal hospitals, and more often than not they own or co-own the practice. Other vets focus on large animals and may spend a good deal of their time at farms, ranches, aquariums, or zoos. Still others may specialize in areas such as surgery, animal optometry, or pathology. Additional opportunities for veterinarians are

Get Ready!
- Choose a college prep track in high school and keep your grades up.
- Consider adopting a pet or volunteering at the local animal shelter.
- Seek out a summer or after-school job in a veterinarian's office or pet store.

Hire Yourself!

You've been hired as a veterinary technician. For your first assignment, your employer, the best veterinarian in town, wants you to prepare a checklist of routine care for both dogs and cats. Use websites like *www.healthypet.com*, *www.cdc.gov/healthypets*, and *http://dogs.about.com/library/weekly* to seek out information.

found in the public health arena, in pharmaceutical research, in pet food and toy manufacturing, and, of course, in veterinary education.

Veterinarians must complete a rigorous training process that begins with obtaining a bachelor's degree and ends with a doctorate in veterinary medicine. The training includes in-depth class and lab studies as well as hands-on experience actually working with animals in a clinical setting.

For animal lovers who prefer a quicker route to the workplace, veterinary technician has become an increasingly popular career option. This occupation requires two years of specialized training and qualifies the veterinary technician to assist vets in many ways, including tending hospitalized patients, conducting routine tests, taking X rays, and assisting in surgeries.

Big Question #5:
do you have the right skills?

Career exploration is, in one sense, career matchmaking. The goal is to match your basic traits, interests and strengths, work values, and work personality with viable career options.

But the "stuff" you bring to a job is only half of the story.

Choosing an ideal job and landing your dream job is a two-way street. Potential employers look for candidates with specific types of skills and backgrounds. This is especially true in our technology-infused, global economy.

In order to find the perfect fit, you need to be fully aware of not only what you've got, but also what prospective employers need.

The following activity is designed to help you accomplish just that. This time we'll use the "wannabe" approach —working with careers you think you want to consider. This same matchmaking process will come in handy when it comes time for the real thing too.

Unfortunately, this isn't one of those "please turn to the end of the chapter and you'll find all the answers" types of activities. This one requires the best critical thinking, problem-solving, and decision-making skills you can muster.

Big Activity #5:
do you have the right skills?

Here's how it works:

Step 1: First, make a chart like the one on page 118.

Step 2: Next, pick a career profile that interests you and use the following resources to compile a list of the traits and skills needed to be successful. Include:

- Information featured in the career profile in this book;
- Information you discover when you look through websites of any of the professional associations or other resources listed with each career profile;
- Information from the career profiles and skills lists found on-line at America's Career InfoNet at **www.acinet.org**.

Briefly list the traits or skills you find on separate lines in the first column of your chart.

Step 3: Evaluate yourself as honestly as possible. If, after careful consideration, you conclude that you already possess one of the traits or skills included on your list, place an *X* in the column marked "Got It!" If you conclude that the skill or trait is one you've yet to acquire, follow these directions to complete the column marked "Get It!":

- If you believe that gaining proficiency in a skill is just a matter of time and experience and you're willing to do whatever it takes to acquire that skill, place a *Y* (for yes) in the corresponding space.
- Or, if you are quite certain that a particular skill is one that you don't possess now, and either can't or won't do what it takes to acquire it, mark the corresponding space with an *N* (for no). For example, you want to be a brain surgeon. It's important, prestigious work and the pay is good. But, truth be told, you'd rather have brain surgery yourself than sit through eight more years of really intense science and math. This rather significant factor may or may not affect your ultimate career choice. But it's better to think it through now rather than six years into med school.

Step 4: Place your completed chart in your Big Question AnswerBook.

When you work through this process carefully, you should get some eye-opening insights into the kinds of careers that are right for you. Half reality check and half wake-up call, this activity lets you see how you measure up against important workforce competencies.

Big Activity #5: **do you have the right skills?**

skill or trait required	got it!	get it!

more
career ideas in
health science

Careers featured in the previous section represent mainstream, highly viable occupations where someone with the right set of skills and training stands more than half a chance of finding gainful employment. However, these ideas are just the beginning. There are lots of ways to make a living in any industry—and this one is no exception.

Following is a list of career ideas related in one way or another to health science. This gigantic list is included here for two reasons. First, to illustrate some unique ways to blend your interests with opportunities. Second, to keep you thinking beyond the obvious.

As you peruse the list you're sure to encounter some occupations you've never heard of before. We hope you get curious enough to look them up. Others may trigger one of those "aha" moments where everything clicks and you know you're onto something good. Either way we hope it helps point the way toward some rewarding opportunities in the health care industry.

Addiction Counselor	Colon & Rectal Surgeon
Allergist	Counselor
Anesthesiologist	Critical Care Physician
Anesthesiologist Assistant	Dental Assistant
Armed Forces Medical Professional	Dental Laboratory Technician
Blood Bank Technologist	Dermatologist
Cardiologist	Developmental Psychologist
Cardiopulmonary Technician	Diagnostic Medical Sonographer
Cardiovascular Technologist	Dietetic Technician
Certified Nurse-Midwife	Dispensing Optician
Clinical Laboratory Scientist	Electrocardiograph Technician
	Emergency Medical Dispatcher

Emergency Physician

Family Physician

General Practitioner

Genetic Counselor

Gerontologist

Health Care Administrator

Health Care Public Relations

Health Educator

Health Information
Administrator

Health Science Librarian

Health Unit Coordinator

Histotechnologist

Histologic Technician

Horticultural Therapist

Immunologist

Internist

Licensed Practical Nurse

Medical Assistant

Medical Coding Specialist

Medical Illustrator

Medical Laboratory
Technician

Medical Photographer

Medical Secretary

Medical Transcriptionist

Medical Writer

Neurological Surgeon

Neurologist

Nuclear Medicine Physician

Nuclear Medicine
Technologist

Nurse Anesthetist

Nurse Practitioner

Nursing Assistant

Nutritionist

Obstetrician and Gynecologist

Occupational Therapy
Assistant

Ophthalmic Medical
Technologist/Technician

Ophthalmologist

Orthopedic Surgeon

Orthotic and Prosthetic
Practitioner

Otolaryngologist

Paramedic

Pathologist

Pediatrician

Perfusionist

Pharmacy Technician

Physical Therapy Assistant

Plastic Surgeon

Podiatrist

Polysomnographic
Technologist

Preventive Medicine
Physician

Psychiatrist

Psychologist

Pulmonologist

Radiation Therapist

Radiologic Technologist

Radiologist

Recreational Therapist

Registered Nurse

Rehabilitation Counselor

Respiratory Therapist

School Nurse

School Psychologist

Social Worker

Sonographer

Speech-Language Pathologist

Surgeon

Surgical Assistant

Surgical Technologist

Therapeutic Recreation
Specialist

Thoracic Surgeon

Urologist

Vascular Surgeon

Vocational-Rehabilitation
Counselor

Big Question #6:
are you on the right path?

You've covered a lot of ground so far. You've had a chance to discover more about your own potential and expectations. You've taken some time to explore the realities of a wide variety of career opportunities within this industry.

Now is a good time to sort through all the details and figure out what all this means to you. This process involves equal measures of input from your head and your heart. Be honest, think big, and, most of all, stay true to you.

You may be considering an occupation that requires years of advanced schooling which, from your point of view, seems an insurmountable hurdle. What do you do? Give up before you even get started? We hope not. We'd suggest that you try some creative thinking.

Big Activity #6:

are you on the right path?

Start by asking yourself if you to want pursue this particular career so badly that you're willing to do whatever it takes to make it. Then stretch your thinking a little to consider alternative routes, nontraditional career paths, and other equally meaningful occupations.

Following are some prompts to help you sort through your ideas. Simply jot down each prompt on a separate sheet of notebook paper and leave plenty of space for your responses.

Big Activity #6: **are you on the right path?**

One thing I know for sure about my future occupation is

I'd prefer to pursue a career that offers

I'd prefer to pursue a career that requires

A career option I'm now considering is

What appeals to me most about this career is

What concerns me most about this career is

Things that I still need to learn about this career include

Big Activity #6: **are you on the right path?**

Another career option I'm considering is

What appeals to me most about this career is

What concerns me most about this career is

Things that I still need to learn about this career include

Of these two career options I've named, the one that best fits most of my interests, skills, values, and work personality is _____ because

At this point in the process, I am

❑ Pretty sure I'm on the right track

❑ Not quite sure yet but still interested in exploring some more

❑ Completely clueless about what I want to do

SECTION 3
experiment with success

Right about now you may find it encouraging to learn that the average person changes careers five to seven times in his or her life. Plus, most college students change majors several times. Even people who are totally set on what they want to do often end up being happier doing something just a little bit different from what they first imagined.

So, whether you think you've found the ultimate answer to career happiness or you're just as confused as ever, you're in good company. The best advice for navigating these important life choices is this: Always keep the door open to new ideas.

As smart and dedicated as you may be, you just can't predict the future. Some of the most successful professionals in any imaginable field could never ever have predicted what—and how—they would be doing what they actually do today. Why? Because when they were in high school those jobs didn't even exist. It was not too long ago that there were no such things as personal computers, Internet research, digital cameras, mass e-mails, cell phones, or any of the other newfangled tools that are so critical to so many jobs today.

Keeping the door open means being open to recognizing changes in yourself as you mature and being open to changes in the way the world works. It also involves a certain willingness to learn new things and tackle new challenges.

It's easy to see how being open to change can sometimes allow you to go further in your chosen career than you ever dreamed. For instance, in almost any profession you can imagine, technology has fueled unprecedented opportunities. Those people and companies who have embraced this "new way of working" have often surpassed their original expectations of success. Just ask Bill Gates. He's now one of the world's wealthiest men thanks to a company called Microsoft that he cofounded while still a student at Harvard University.

It's a little harder to see, but being open to change can also mean that you may have to let go of your first dream and find a more appropriate one. Maybe your dream is to become a professional athlete. At this point in your life you may think that there's nothing in the world that would possibly make you happier. Maybe you're right and maybe you have the talent and persistence (and the lucky breaks) to take you all the way.

But maybe you don't. Perhaps if you opened yourself to new ideas you'd discover that the best career involves blending your interest in sports with your talent in writing to become a sports journalist or sports information director. Maybe your love of a particular sport and your interest in working with children might best be served in a coaching career. Who knows what you might achieve when you open yourself to all the possibilities?

So, whether you've settled on a career direction or you are still not sure where you want to go, there are several "next steps" to consider. In this section, you'll find three more Big Questions to help keep your career planning moving forward. These Big Questions are:

❓ Big Question #7: **who knows what you need to know?**

❓ Big Question #8: **how can you find out what a career is really like?**

❓ Big Question #9: **how do you know when you've made the right choice?**

who knows what you need to know?

When it comes to the nitty-gritty details about what a particular job is really like, who knows what you need to know? Someone with a job like the one you want, of course. They'll have the inside scoop—important information you may never find in books or websites. So make talking to as many people as you can part of your career planning process.

Learn from them how they turned their own challenges into opportunities, how they got started, and how they made it to where they are now. Ask the questions that aren't covered in "official" resources, such as what it is really like to do their job, how they manage to do a good job and have a great life, how they learned what they needed to learn to do their job well, and the best companies or situations to start in.

A good place to start with these career chats or "informational interviews" is with people you know—or more likely, people you know who know people with jobs you find interesting. People you already know include your parents (of course), relatives, neighbors, friends' parents, people who belong to your place of worship or club, and so on.

All it takes to get the process going is gathering up all your nerve and asking these people for help. You'll find that nine and a half times out of 10, the people you encounter will be delighted to help, either by providing information about their careers or by introducing you to people they know who can help.

hints and tips for a successful interview

●TIP #1

Think about your goals for the interview, and write them down.

Be clear about what you want to know after the interview that you didn't know before it.

Remember that the questions for all personal interviews are not the same. You would probably use different questions to write a biography of the person, to evaluate him or her for a job, to do a history of the industry, or to learn about careers that might interest you.

Writing down your objectives will help you stay focused.

●TIP #2

Pay attention to how you phrase your questions.

Some questions that we ask people are "closed" questions; we are looking for a clear answer, not an elaboration. "What time does the movie start?" is a good example of a closed question.

Sometimes, when we ask a closed question, we shortchange ourselves. Think about the difference between "What times are the showings tonight?" and "Is there a 9 P.M. showing?" By asking the second question, you may not find out if there is an 8:45 or 9:30 show.

That can be frustrating. It usually seems so obvious when we ask a question that we expect a full answer. It's important to remember, though, that the person hearing the question doesn't always have the same priorities or know why the question is being asked.

The best example of this? Think of the toddler who answers the phone. When the caller asks, "Is your mom home?" the toddler says, "Yes" and promptly hangs up. Did the child answer the question? As far as he's concerned, he did a great job!

Another problem with closed questions is that they sometimes require so many follow-up questions that the person being interviewed feels like a suspect in an interrogation room.

A series of closed questions may go this way:

Q: What is your job title?
A: Assistant Producer
Q: How long have you had that title?
A: About two years.

Q: What was your title before that?
Q: How long did you have that title?
Q: What is the difference between the two jobs?
Q: What did you do before that?
Q: Where did you learn to do this job?
Q: How did you advance from one job to the next?

An alternative, "open" question invites conversation. An open-question interview might begin this way:

I understand you are an Assistant Producer. I'm really interested in what that job is all about and how you got to be at the level you are today.

Open questions often begin with words like:

Tell me about . . .
How do you feel about . . .
What was it like . . .

● TIP #3

Make the person feel comfortable answering truthfully.
In general, people don't want to say things that they think will make them look bad. How to get at the truth? Be empathic, and make their answers seem "normal."

Ask a performer or artist how he or she feels about getting a bad review from the critics, and you are unlikely to hear, "It really hurts. Sometimes I just want to cry and get out of the business." Or "Critics are so stupid. They never understand what I am trying to do."

Try this approach instead: "So many people in your industry find it hard to deal with the hurt of a bad critical review. How do you handle it when that happens?"

ask the experts

You can learn a lot by interviewing people who are already successful in the types of careers you're interested in. In fact, we followed our own advice and interviewed several people who have been successful in the health sciences field to share with you here.

Before you get started on your own interview, take a few minutes to look through the results of some of ours. To make it easier for you to compare the responses of all the people we interviewed, we have presented our interviews as a panel discussion that reveals important success lessons these people have learned along the way. Each panelist is introduced on the next page.

Our interviewees gave us great information about things like what their jobs are really like, how they got to where they are, and even provided a bit of sage advice for people like you who are just getting started.

So Glad You Asked

In addition to the questions we asked in the interviews in this book, you might want to add some of these questions to your own interviews:

- How did your childhood interests relate to your choice of career path?
- How did you first learn about the job you have today?
- In what ways is your job different from how you expected it to be?
- Tell me about the parts of your job that you really like.
- If you could get someone to take over part of your job for you, what aspect would you most like to give up?
- If anything were possible, how would you change your job description?
- What kinds of people do you usually meet in your work?
- Walk me through the whole process of getting your type of product made and distributed. Tell me about all the people who are involved.
- Tell me about the changes you have seen in your industry over the years. What do you see as the future of the industry?
- Are there things you would do differently in your career if you could do it all over?

real people with real jobs in health science

Following are introductions to our panel of experts. Get acquainted with their backgrounds and then use their job titles to track their stories throughout the eight success lessons.

- **Clinical Pharmacist Dr. Peter Anderson** works at a state hospital in Quincy, Massachusetts.
- **Speech Pathologist Jan Braverman** works with students at the Hebrew Academy of Cleveland in Ohio.
- **Dr. John Cho** is a **Cardiothoracic Surgeon** and army officer serving at Walter Reed Army Hospital and commander of Andrew Rader U.S. Army Health Clinic in Potomac, Maryland.
- **Acupuncturist Dr. Marc Cutler** uses traditional Chinese medicine and herbal remedies to care for patients in Raleigh, North Carolina.
- **Dr. Tammi Davis** is a self-employed **Family Physician** and medical acupuncturist who practices in Owings Mills, Maryland.
- **Dr. Brett Finkelstein** is a **Veterinarian** who directs a small animal veterinary hospital in Safety Harbor, Florida.
- **Nurse Practitioner Patricia Kennedy** works in a mental health agency in Tempe, Arizona.
- **Aly Khan** travels the world fighting disease as a **Medical Epidemiologist** for the Centers for Disease Control and Prevention. He is based in Atlanta, Georgia.
- **Occupational Therapist Alexander Minevich** works in Kennesaw, Georgia.
- **Massage Therapist Anthony Mirabel** works in Stamford, Connecticut, where he owns a practice called The Kneaded Touch.
- **Optometrist Dr. Michael Peters** is currently a practicing partner of Eye Care Associates in Raleigh, North Carolina. He blends his love of sports with his skills as an optometrist by working as a team eye doctor for the NHL Carolina Hurricanes, the Tampa Bay Devil Ray's baseball players through their Triple-A team in Durham, North Carolina, and a wide variety of local professional and amateur athletes.

Jan Braverman

Dr. John Cho

Dr. Marc Cutler

Dr. Tammi Davis

Dr. Michael Peters

Success Lesson #1:
Work is a good thing when you find the right career.

- **Tell us what it's like to work in your current career.**

Nurse Practitioner: My main responsibilities are diagnosing mental illnesses like depression, obsessive-compulsive disorder, eating disorders, and schizophrenia (to name just a few) and then prescribing medication that will help the person, then monitoring the person for the effects of the medication. On a typical day I will see 10 to 14 people for about 20 to 30 minutes each to see how they are doing and adjust their medications. I work in a hospital one day a week and in a clinic the other days. A great thing about my profession is that it is very flexible and very much in demand right now in my area. States differ in what they allow nurse practitioners to do, so the flexibility and demand may be different in other states.

Family Physician: I provided clinical primary care for 11 years. But now I work at a local college in the student health center where I oversee the nurse practitioners and examine, diagnose, and treat the students for a variety of medical conditions. I also provide counseling, preventative health, and care for injuries. I really love working with adolescents and young adults.

In addition, I have a part-time acupuncture practice, which is very different from traditional western medicine. I have been quite impressed with the results, treating such problems as back/neck pain, headaches, insomnia, anxiety, and shoulder/knee pain. I really enjoy this as well, especially since I can spend an hour with each patient, which is something that one cannot usually do when practicing traditional primary care medicine.

Clinical Pharmacist: My main job is working as a clinical pharmacist in a state psychiatric hospital. I don't do any dispensing of medications. I help medical doctors (mostly psychiatrists) select the best medication to treat the patients with. I also educate physicians, nurses, and patients about medications. I serve as chairperson for the Research Steering Committee. This committee oversees all research in the hospital. I also work as a forensic pharmacist in a private consulting practice. This provides medico-legal consults for attorneys. For example, I may be asked to offer an opinion as to whether an injury was caused by a certain drug. I have been consulted on cases relating to malpractice, sexual assault, worker's compensation, fraud, and drunk driving. I also do much writing both as part of my main job and as a consultant.

Everybody has to start somewhere!

Following is a list of first jobs once held by our esteemed panel of experts.

Waitress/Waiter

Child care provider

Camp counselor

Stock girl

Busboy

Landscaper

Pizza maker

School bus driver

Tax preparer

Tutor

Massage Therapist: It's all about service; if you are not willing to be understanding to your clients and willing to bend and twist for them you will go hungry. This is where my bartending and waiting experience came in handy. When you have to work for tips, you learn what service is all about.

Cardiothoracic Surgeon: I was recently chief of surgery for the 212th MASH (mobile army surgical hospital), and we were deployed in support of Operation Iraqi Freedom in central Iraq. My job at Walter Reed Army Medical center is as a pediatric and adult cardiothoracic surgeon. I am also the commander of the Rader Clinic. The U.S. Army provides a myriad of opportunities to allow a physician to stay professionally challenged.

Occupational Therapist: I work with children with special needs, both cognitive and physical. I work on not only rehabilitating them to regain old skills but also by helping them learn new ones. I work on such things as strengthening and building endurance. Also, I get to "play" for a living. We ride bicycles, build obstacle courses, and even bake cakes. We also work on drawing and other school-related activities.

When I'm not visiting clients, I'm busy documenting my client visits so that my colleagues and I can keep track of who our agency has served and what it is we have provided for our clients. I also go to meetings and I participate in brainstorming sessions that look at how our department can improve and continue to grow. Lastly, I mentor occupational therapy students who are on their three-month fieldwork experience.

Acupuncturist: My job is to help people keep their bodies in a state of optimal health. I use acupuncture, herbal medicine, and other modalities to guide the body to balance.

Optometrist: I check people's eyes to see if they need glasses or contacts. I also check the health of their eyes to make sure there are no diseases present that cause blindness, such as glaucoma, macular degeneration, and diabetes. If these are present, I refer people to eye surgeons to help correct these problems. I also treat people with eye injuries and infections. With children, we test the visual system to make sure that the eye muscles and focusing system are working properly for learning. If there is a deficiency, we offer vision therapy to improve those areas. These are exercises that allow the visual system to work better at getting the information to the brain and then process that information correctly. For athletes, we have similar exercises that can help eye/hand/body coordination and mental preparation. For people that are visually impaired, we have devices, such as magnifiers and telescopes, that can improve sight.

Medical Epidemiologist: I investigate infectious disease outbreaks all over the world to help develop controls measures for affected communities and to help prevent disease in unaffected areas. Most recently I participated in efforts to control the SARS outbreak in Singapore and the monkeypox outbreak in Indiana. When I am not in the field, I help review our infectious disease research activities and promote our government's international health programs.

Veterinarian: I direct a small animal veterinary hospital comprising veterinarians, receptionists, technicians, and lay help. Our job is to provide medical and support services to our community pets and their owners. I wear many hats each day. I am an administrator one minute, a surgeon the next, and a bereavement counselor following that. The diversity and the challenges of daily practice life keep me on my toes and motivated.

Success Lesson #2:
Career goals change and so do you.

- ## How did you end up doing what you're now doing?

Nurse Practitioner: I worked as a registered nurse for many years in psychiatric hospitals. A person must be a nurse first before they can become a nurse practitioner.

Speech Pathologist: Just being in the right place at the right time. It was helpful to meet as many people as possible in different settings because many of these people would later become referral sources.

Family Physician: I first worked for an urgent care center, then joined a multispecialty medical group and stayed there for six years. My next job was with a group primary care practice where I got lots of clinical experience.

Massage Therapist: Believe it or not, working with the public as a bartender and waiter helped prepare me for this work.

Occupational Therapist: Tutoring other students in study skills helped me better understand learning disabilities and physical difficulties.

Acupuncturist: Some inner drive seemed to direct me to this field. I had other jobs such as counseling, peer tutoring, and student leadership positions in college where I discovered that my life's work had to involve helping people in some way.

Optometrist: I had to start wearing glasses in the second grade. As a teenager, I had problems wearing contact lenses while playing sports. I decided that I would like to be able to help people who had similar problems achieving life goals because of their visual situations.

Medical Epidemiologist: I got lots of support from my family and friends. All my early jobs led to where I am now at the Centers for Disease Control (CDC).

Veterinarian: I had always dreamt of becoming a veterinarian and owning my own companion animal hospital. Great mentors along the way guided me and helped me to keep my dream alive, even when times were tough. I am forever indebted to these individuals who allowed me the opportunity to learn about my chosen path as I traveled through my career development.

Success Lesson #3:
There are good and bad parts to every job.

- ### What do you especially like about your job?
  Nurse Practitioner: I get to help people every day who feel bad. I give them hope and I get to teach them something or give some helpful advice. I listen to their problems and let them know I care about them. I prescribe medication to help decrease their symptoms. They usually feel better when they leave my office, and sometimes they return to normal.

  Acupuncturist: The best part of my job is working with people and seeing the results.

- ### Your least favorite parts of your job?
  Nurse Practitioner: The worst thing about my job is having people that never really get any better in spite of what I do.

Acupuncturist: At this point I really don't have a worst part. When I get up in the morning I know my purpose and whatever happens at the office is okay.

Success Lesson #4:
There's more than one way to get an education.

- **Where did you learn the skills of your field, both formally (school) and informally (experience)?**

Nurse Practitioner: A master's degree in nursing with a special emphasis on being a psychiatric nurse practitioner is required. A desire to help other people and being absolutely fascinated with psychology and behavior is essential. Most psychiatric patients have had bad life experiences, like abuse and abandonment, so empathy, and an ability to hear and not be depressed by such things is needed. All my life experiences prepared me for this job—especially the bad ones!

Speech Pathologist: A master's degree is a necessity. It is helpful to have good writing and communication skills.

Family Physician: It took four years of college, four years of medical school, and a three-year residency to become a family physician. You need to get great grades and be well rounded in extracurricular activities to get into a good school. You must be good at memorizing, quick to understand concepts, and you must have a desire to help people and be able to empathize and understand people. You must be a good communicator and be very patient and a good listener. You need to make people feel confident in your abilities, and you must have a good sense of humor.

Massage Therapist: Therapy school, business school, and 12 years in the restaurant business.

Clinical Pharmacist: I've earned a bachelor's of science degree in pharmacy and a Doctor of Pharmacy degree. My personality traits include creativity, ambition, and the ability to see the "big picture."

Cardiothoracic Surgeon: I received additional subspecialty training at Walter Reed and the Mayo Clinic. Ability is important in my specialty. I would say though that flexibility and initiative are important traits for a successful army surgeon.

Occupational Therapist: I started with a background in child psychology and have a love of working with kids and parents. Academically, one especially needs an understanding of anatomy and basic health sciences as well as business-related interests.

Success Lesson #5:
Good choices and hard work are a potent combination.

● **What are you most proud of in your career?**

Nurse Practitioner: When I get patients who are extremely mentally ill and give them medication that returns them to normal, it is very gratifying.

Speech Pathologist: I started a private practice with two other speech pathologists and we were known throughout Cleveland. We had contracts with hospitals, nursing homes, and schools.

Family Physician: In the past 13 years of medical practice, I have had many accomplishments. Making correct diagnoses and getting patients feeling better is very rewarding. I have been very successful with the acupuncture and have helped many people with their pain problems when other types of traditional medicine (pain medications, neurology consults, surgery, nerve blocks, etc.) had failed.

My most important accomplishment however, is being a mom. I make sure that I work my schedule around my kids, so that I can be there for them—my kids give me the most pleasure of all.

Massage Therapist: Opening the doors for the Kneaded Touch and being in business for almost six years now.

Clinical Pharmacist: Several things come to mind. One is being appointed guest editor for the *Journal of Pharmacy Practice* for an issue devoted to forensics. Another achievement was being appointed director of the division of pharmacology by the American College of Forensic Examiners, the world's largest forensic association.

Cardiothoracic Surgeon: I would say that utilizing my skills as a cardiothoracic surgeon in Iraq has been the most rewarding experience to me thus far. It was great to provide lifesaving care to the soldiers of this great country.

Occupational Therapist: I have taught many kids to tie laces, ride bikes, learn to maintain their balance, learn how to stay focused in school, and how to develop strength in their bodies. I have helped parents learn that their child is special and how to build on their strengths and compensate for their weaknesses.

Doctor of Oriental Medicine: I have seen many people who would not have tried this ancient medicine give it a go and have tremendous results.

Optometrist: I have kept several people from going blind by treating their glaucoma. I have helped many athletes make it to professional status and keep that status. I have helped many children erase their learning problems by correcting weaknesses in their visual system.

Medical Epidemiologist: During the 1995 outbreak of Ebola, I was able to use epidemiology methods to trace back the first case and prove that the hundreds of cases were all linked to one person. During a 1997 outbreak of monkeypox, a disease similar to smallpox, my team was able to determine that the outbreak was expected and did not mean that we needed to resume smallpox vaccination.

Veterinarian: My most exciting accomplishment so far does not entail a veterinary-related activity. It is raising my two wonderful beautiful children. However, as a veterinarian I think being a caring, competent, compassionate practitioner makes every day a great day in my practice.

Success Lesson #6:
It really isn't just what you know.

- **Are there any people who especially helped you in your career?**

    Nurse Practitioner: My husband suggested nursing, which I had never thought of. After I looked into it I thought it sounded good because it had the flexibility I needed to be with my family, and

I wanted to help people. There was no such thing as a nurse practitioner back then, I don't think. I first got my associate's degree, and then began working on my bachelor's degree. It took many years to get it. By the time I was ready for my master's, there was a psych nurse practitioner program, which I entered.

Speech Pathologist: My college counselor.

Family Physician: I saw that traditional medicine was unable to help with all problems. Many times patients are told that nothing more can be done for them or they are told that their problems are just psychological. I researched use of acupuncture for various problems and was very impressed. So I studied medical acupuncture through UCLA Medical School.

Clinical Pharmacist: My teachers and my family influenced me most. Reading books on science and criminal justice helped inspire my choices.

Massage Therapist: When my father passed away it was all about health. He did not take care of himself and I knew I needed to take care of myself. At that point I decided to go to massage therapy school and get my license for massage.

Cardiothoracic Surgeon: While still a student at the United States Military Academy I worked with a number of surgeons.

Occupational Therapist: When I was younger, I was taken to see Professor Harvey Mandel at York University's Center for Achievement and Motivation (Toronto, Ontario, Canada). He was the first person who listened to me and told me I was good at something.

Acupuncturist: People in my family who had illnesses that were not helped by traditional allopathic medicines led me to investigate alternative medicines.

Medical Epidemiologist: I became interested in infectious diseases after reading a book about Louis Pasteur. His work on the germ theory and advances in pasteurization and vaccination without any sophisticated equipment was amazing. He inspired me to a life of investigation.

Veterinarian: The first veterinarian who employed me was a man named Walter Relken who owned a small animal hospital in Queens, New York. He always had a smile on his face and a life lesson on his mind. I was in my senior year in high school when I began working for him. To this day I credit him with helping me to become the veterinarian I am.

Success Lesson #7:
You can learn from other people's mistakes.

- **Is there anything you wish you had done differently?**

    Family Physician: I wish I had studied acupuncture earlier so that I could have integrated it into my practice years ago.

    Occupational Therapist: I wish I had taken more courses on how to run your own business. There is so much room to start your own business. It's hard to learn these skills outside of school.

Success Lesson #8:
A little advice goes a long way.

- **What advice do you have for a young person just getting started?**

    Nurse Practitioner: I would encourage anyone who is considering nursing to go straight for the bachelor's degree and not the associate's degree. Find out if you are a "psych" person or not—people either love it or hate it. There are many other kinds of nurse practitioners also: pediatric, family, ob-gyn, adult, geriatric. If money is important to you, go to medical school instead and become a physician. They make more money for similar work.

Speech Pathologist: You must be willing to get your gratification from helping people rather than earning a lot of money! You must have compassion and a great deal of patience.

Massage Therapist: Service, service, service. Pay attention to details and be prepared for long hours.

Clinical Pharmacist: Take courses in biology, chemistry, and physics.

Cardiothoracic Surgeon: In my opinion, one should be able to look back at the end of a career and see that the fruits of his or her labor have provided a service to the community or improved the lives of others. As an army surgeon, you can say both. Our soldiers in the Armed Services deserve the best care possible. This is the least we can offer to those who put their lives on the line to serve this nation.

Occupational Therapist: This is one of the top 10 career areas with respect to growth and demand. You will never be out of work and will feel like you are helping others. Take some time and volunteer at different centers (age groups and disabilities). Learn about this job field because one day you'll feel like it's a great way to not only make a living but also a great way to live. You will come home feeling like you made a difference.

Acupuncturist: Pursue your passion. My career choice is not in the mainstreatm. I spend most of my time educating people about what I do. If you love working with people and want to make a difference in the human condition then by all means consider alternative medicine.

Optometrist: I would advise students to look up an optometry school on-line to get an idea if they feel like this is a correct path and that the workload to achieve this goal is something that is appropriate for them. Then, I would recommend that they contact their local eye doctor and ask to shadow the doctor for a day. This will give them a great snapshot of what to expect.

Medical Epidemiologist: Communicate with people to get a sense of what they do. Most scientists are delighted to communicate with young people and one of them may become a lifelong mentor. Take lots of science and math courses. Most importantly, enjoy it. Science is fun!

Veterinarian: Take the time to explore the many avenues available to you in veterinary medicine. Not everyone becomes a small animal practitioner. There are wonderful opportunities in public health, research, pharmaceuticals, and teaching. Explore them all and find the right fit.

Also, do well in school and be sure to study a broad spectrum of subjects and disciplines. They will all come in handy as you prepare to enter your chosen field.

Big Activity #7:
who knows what you need to know?

It's one thing to read about conducting an informational interview, but it's another thing altogether to actually do one. Now it's your turn to shine. Just follow these steps for doing it like a pro!

Step 1: Identify the people you want to talk to about their work.

Step 2: Set up a convenient time to meet in person or talk over the phone.

Step 3: Make up a list of questions that reflect things you'd really like to know about that person's work. Go for the open questions you just read about.

Step 4: Talk away! Take notes as your interviewee responds to each question.

Step 5: Use your notes to write up a "news" article that describes the person and his or her work.

Step 6: Place all your notes and the finished "news" article in your Big Question AnswerBook.

Big Activity #7: **who knows what you need to know?**

contact information	appointments/sample questions
name	day time
company	location
title	
address	
	sample questions:
phone	
email	
name	day time
company	location
title	
address	
	sample questions:
phone	
email	
name	day time
company	location
title	
address	
	sample questions:
phone	
email	

experiment with success   **143**

Big Activity #7: **who knows what you need to know?**

questions	answers

INTERVIEW NOTES

Big Activity #7: **who knows what you need to know?**

questions	answers

INTERVIEW NOTES

Big Activity #7: **who knows what you need to know?**

NEWS

Big Activity #7: **who knows what you need to know?**

NEWS

Big Question #8:

how can you find out what a career is really like?

There are some things you just have to figure out for yourself. Things like whether your interest in pursuing a career in marine biology is practical if you plan to live near the Mojave Desert.

Other things you have to see for yourself. Words are sometimes not enough when it comes to conveying what a job is really like on a day-to-day basis—what it looks like, sounds like, and feels like.

Here are a few ideas for conducting an on-the-job reality check.

identify typical types of workplaces

Think of all the places that jobs like the ones you like take place. Almost all of the careers in this book, or ones very similar to them, exist in the corporate world, in the public sector, and in the military. And don't forget the option of going into business for yourself!

For example: Are you interested in public relations? You can find a place for yourself in almost any sector of our economy. Of course, companies definitely want to promote their products. But don't limit yourself to the Fortune 500 corporate world. Hospitals, schools, and manufacturers need your services. Cities, states, and even countries also need your services. They want to increase tourism, get businesses to relocate there, and convince workers to live there or students to study there. Each military branch needs to recruit new members and to show how they are using the money they receive from the government for medical research, taking care of families, and other non-news-breaking uses. Charities, community organizations, and even religious groups want to promote the good things they are doing so that they will get more members, volunteers, contributions, and funding. Political candidates, parties, and special interest groups all want to promote their messages. Even actors, dancers, and writers need to promote themselves.

Not interested in public relations but know you want a career that involves lots of writing? You've thought about becoming the more obvious choices—novelist, newspaper reporter, or English teacher. But you don't want to overlook other interesting possibilities, do you?

What if you also enjoy technical challenges? Someone has to write the documentation for all those computer games and software.

Love cars? Someone has to write those owner's manuals too.

Ditto on those government reports about safety and environmental standards for industries.

Maybe community service is your thing. You can mix your love for helping people with writing grant proposals seeking funds for programs at hospitals, day care centers, or rehab centers.

Talented in art and design? Those graphics you see in magazine advertisements, on your shampoo bottle, and on a box of cereal all have to be created by someone.

That someone could be you.

find out about the job outlook

Organizations like the U.S. Bureau of Labor Statistics spend a lot of time and energy gathering data on what kinds of jobs are most in demand now and what kinds are projected to be in demand in the future. Find out what the job outlook is for a career you like. A good resource for this data can be found on-line at America's Career InfoNet at *www.acinet.org/acinet.*

This information will help you understand whether the career options you find most appealing are viable. In other words, job outlook data will give you a better sense of your chances of actually finding gainful employment in your chosen profession—a rather important consideration from any standpoint.

Be realistic. You may really, really want to be a film critic at a major newspaper. Maybe your ambition is to become the next Roger Ebert.

Think about this. How many major newspapers are there? Is it reasonable to pin all your career hopes on a job for which there are only about 10 positions in the whole country? That doesn't mean that it's impossible to achieve your ambition. After all, someone has to fill those positions. It should just temper your plans with realism and perhaps encourage you to have a back-up plan, just in case.

look at training requirements

Understand what it takes to prepare yourself for a specific job. Some jobs require only a high school diploma. Others require a couple of years of technical training, while still others require four years or more in college.

Be sure to investigate a variety of training options. Look at training programs and colleges you may like to attend. Check out their websites to see what courses are required for the major you want. Make sure you're willing to "do the time" in school to prepare yourself for a particular occupation.

experiment with success

see for yourself

There's nothing quite like seeing for yourself what a job is like. Talk with a teacher or guidance counselor to arrange a job-shadowing opportunity with someone who is in the job or in a similar one.

Job shadowing is an activity that involves actually spending time at work with someone to see what a particular job is like up close and personal. It's an increasingly popular option and your school may participate in specially designated job-shadowing days. For some especially informative resources on job shadowing, visit **www.jobshadow.org**.

Another way to test-drive different careers is to find summer jobs and internships that are similar to the career you hope to pursue.

make a Plan B

Think of the alternatives! Often it's not possible to have a full-time job in the field you love. Some jobs just don't pay enough to meet the needs of every person or family. Maybe you recognize that you don't have the talent, drive, or commitment to rise to the top. Or, perhaps you can't afford the years of work it takes to get established or you place a higher priority on spending time with family than that career might allow.

If you can see yourself in any of those categories, DO NOT GIVE UP on what you love! There is always more than one way to live out your dreams. Look at some of the other possibilities in this book. Find a way to integrate your passion into other jobs or your free time.

Lots of people manage to accomplish this in some fairly impressive ways. For instance, the Knicks City Dancers, known for their incredible performances and for pumping up the crowd at Knicks basketball games, include an environmental engineer, a TV news assignment editor, and a premed student, in addition to professional dancers. The Broadband Pickers, a North Texas bluegrass band, is made up of five lawyers and one businessman. In fact, even people who are extremely successful in a field that they love find ways to indulge their other passions. Paul Newman, the actor and director, not only drives race cars as a hobby, but also produces a line of gourmet foods and donates the profits to charity.

Get the picture? Good. Hang in there and keep moving forward in your quest to find your way toward a great future.

Big Activity #8:
how can you find out
what a career is really like?

This activity will help you conduct a reality check about your future career in two ways. First, it prompts you to find out more about the nitty-gritty details you really need to know to make a well-informed career choice. Second, it helps you identify strategies for getting a firsthand look at what it's like to work in a given profession—day in and day out.

Here's how to get started:

Step 1: Write the name of the career you're considering at the top of a sheet of paper (or use the following worksheets if this is your book).

Step 2: Create a checklist (or, if this is your book, use the one provided on the following pages) covering two types of reality-check items.

First, list four types of information to investigate:
- training requirements
- typical workplaces
- job outlook
- similar occupations

Second, list three types of opportunities to pursue:
- job shadowing
- apprenticeship
- internship

Step 3: Use resources such as America's Career InfoNet at ***www. acinet. org*** and Career OneStop at ***www.careeronestop.org*** to seek out the information you need.

Step 4: Make an appointment with your school guidance counselor to discuss how to pursue hands-on opportunities to learn more about this occupation. Use the space provided on the following worksheets to jot down preliminary contact information and a brief summary of why or why not each career is right for you.

Step 5: When you're finished, place these notes in your Big Question AnswerBook.

Big Activity #8: **how can you find out**
what a career is really like?

career choice:	
training requirements	
typical workplaces	
job outlook	
similar occupations	

INFORMATION

Big Activity #8: **how can you find out what a career is really like?**

job shadowing	when:
	where:
	who:
	observations and impressions:

apprenticeship	when:
	where:
	who:
	observations and impressions:

internship	when:
	where:
	who:
	observations and impressions:

OPPORTUNITIES

Big Question #9:

how do you know when you've made the right choice?

When it comes right down to it, finding the career that's right for you is like shopping in a mall with 12,000 different stores. Finding the right fit may require trying on lots of different options.

All the Big Questions you've answered so far have been designed to expand your career horizons and help you clarify what you really want in a career. The next step is to see how well you've managed to integrate your interests, capabilities, goals, and ambitions with the realities of specific opportunities.

There are two things for you to keep in mind as you do this.

First, recognize the value of all the hard work you did to get to this point. If you've already completed the first eight activities thoughtfully and honestly, whatever choices you make will be based on solid knowledge about yourself and your options. You've learned to use a process that works just as well now, when you're trying to get an inkling of what you want to do with your life, as it will later when you have solid job offers on the table and need to make decisions that will affect your life and family.

Second, always remember that sometimes, even when you do everything right, things don't turn out the way you'd planned. That's called life. It happens. And it's not the end of the world. Even if you make what seems to be a bad choice, know this—there's no such thing as a wasted experience. The paths you take, the training you receive, the people you meet—they ultimately fall together like puzzle pieces to make you who you are and prepare you for what you're meant to do.

That said, here's a strategy to help you confirm that you are making the very best choices you can.

Big Activity #9:
how do you know when you've made the right choice?

One way to confirm that the choices you are making are right for you is to look at both sides of this proverbial coin: what you are looking for and what each career offers. The following activity will help you think this through.

Step 1: To get started, make two charts with four columns (or, if this is your book, use the following worksheets).

Step 2: Label the first column of the first chart as "Yes Please!" Under this heading list all the qualities you absolutely must have in a future job. This might include factors such as the kind of training you'd prefer to pursue (college, apprenticeship, etc.); the type of place where you'd like to work (big office, high-tech lab, in the great outdoors, etc.); and the sorts of people you want to work with (children, adults, people with certain needs, etc.). It may also include salary requirements or dress code preferences.

Step 3: Now at the top of the next three columns write the names of three careers you are considering. (This is a little like Big Activity #3 where you examined your work values. But now you know a lot more and you're ready to zero in on specific careers.)

Step 4: Go down the list and use an *X* to indicate careers that do indeed feature the desired preferences. Use an *O* to indicate those that do not.

Step 5: Tally up the number of *Xs* and *Os* at the bottom of each career column to find out which comes closest to your ideal job.

Step 6: In the first column of the second chart add a heading called "No Thanks!" This is where you'll record the factors you simply prefer not to deal with. Maybe long hours, physically demanding work, or jobs that require years of advanced training just don't cut it for you. Remember that part of figuring out what you do want to do involves understanding what you don't want to do.

Step 7: Repeat steps 2 through 5 for these avoid-at-all-costs preferences as you did for the must-have preferences above.

Big Activity #9: **how do you know when you've made the right choice?**

yes please!	career #1	career #2	career #3
totals	__X__O	__X__O	__X__O

Big Activity #9: **how do you know when you've made the right choice?**

no thanks!	career #1	career #2	career #3
totals	__X__O	__X__O	__X__O

? Big Question #10:
what's next?

Think of this experience as time well invested in your future. And expect it to pay off in a big way down the road. By now, you have worked (and perhaps wrestled) your way through nine important questions:

- ? Big Question #1: **who are you?**
- ? Big Question #2: **what are your interests and strengths?**
- ? Big Question #3: **what are your work values?**
- ? Big Question #4: **what is your work personality?**
- ? Big Question #5: **do you have the right skills?**
- ? Big Question #6: **are you on the right path?**
- ? Big Question #7: **who knows what you need to know?**
- ? Big Question #8: **how can you find out what a career is really like?**
- ? Big Question #9: **how do you know when you've made the right choice?**

But what if you still don't have a clue about what you want to do with your life?

Don't worry. You're talking about one of the biggest life decisions you'll ever make. These things take time.

It's okay if you don't have all the definitive answers yet. At least you do know how to go about finding them. The process you've used to work through this book is one that you can rely on throughout your life to help you sort through the options and make sound career decisions.

So what's next?

More discoveries, more exploration, and more experimenting with success are what come next. Keep at it and you're sure to find your way to wherever your dreams and ambitions lead you.

And, just for good measure, here's one more Big Activity to help point you in the right direction.

Big Activity #10:
what's next?

List five things you can do to move forward in your career planning process (use a separate sheet if you need to). Your list may include tasks such as talking to your guidance counselor about resources your school makes available, checking out colleges or other types of training programs that can prepare you for your life's work, or finding out about job-shadowing or internship opportunities in your community. Remember to include any appropriate suggestions from the Get Started Now! list included with each career profile in Section 2 of this book.

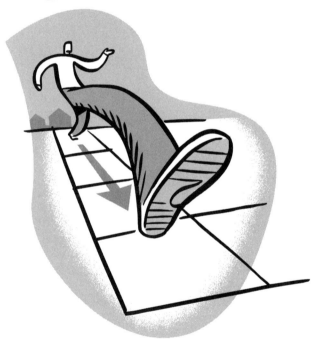

experiment with success

Big Activity #10: **what's next?**

career planning to-do list

1

2

3

4

5

a final word

You are now officially equipped with the tools you need to track down a personally appropriate profession any time you have the need or desire. You've discovered more about who you are and what you want. You've explored a variety of career options within a very important industry. You've even taken it upon yourself to experiment with what it might be like to actually work in certain occupations.

Now it's up to you to put all this newfound knowledge to work for you. While you're at it, here's one more thing to keep in mind: Always remember that there's no such thing as a wasted experience. Certainly some experiences are more positive than others, but they all teach us something.

Chances are you may not get everything right the first time out. It may turn out that you were incorrect about how much you would love to go to a certain college or pursue a particular profession. That doesn't mean you're doomed to failure. It simply means that you've lived and learned. Sometimes you just won't know for sure about one direction or another until you try things out a bit. Nothing about your future has to be written in stone. Allow yourself some freedom to experiment with various options until you find something that really clicks for you.

Figuring out what you want to do with the rest of your life is a big deal. It's probably one of the most exciting and among the most intimidating decisions you'll ever make. It's a decision that warrants clear-headed thought and wholehearted investigation. It's a process that's likely to take you places you never dared imagine if you open yourself up to all the possibilities. Take a chance on yourself and seek out and follow your most valued hopes and dreams into the workplace.

Best wishes for a bright future!

Appendix

a virtual support team

As you continue your quest to determine just what it is you want to do with your life, you'll find that you are not alone. There are many people and organizations who want to help you succeed. Here are two words of advice—let them! Take advantage of all the wonderful resources so readily available to you.

The first place to start is your school's guidance center. There you are quite likely to find a variety of free resources which include information about careers, colleges, and other types of training opportunities; details about interesting events, job shadowing activities, and internship options; and access to useful career assessment tools.

In addition, since you are the very first generation on the face of the earth to have access to a world of information just the click of a mouse away—use it! The following Internet resources provide all kinds of information and ideas that can help you find your future.

make an informed choice

Following are five of the very best career-oriented websites currently on-line. Be sure to bookmark these websites and visit them often as you consider various career options.

America's Career Info Net *www.acinet.org/acinet/default.asp*

Quite possibly the most comprehensive source of career exploration anywhere, this U.S. Department of Labor website includes all kinds of current information about wages, market conditions, employers, and employment trends. Make sure to visit the site's career video library where you'll find links to over 450 videos featuring real people doing real jobs.

Careers & Colleges *www.careersandcolleges.com*

Each year Careers & Colleges publishes four editions of *Careers & Colleges* magazine, designed to help high school students set and meet their academic, career, and financial goals. Ask your guidance counselor about receiving free copies. You'll also want to visit the excellent Careers and Colleges website. Here you'll encounter their "Virtual Guidance Counselor," an interactive career database that allows you to match your interests with college majors or careers that are right for you.

Career Voyages *www.careervoyages.gov*

This website is brought to you compliments of collaboration between the U.S. Department of Labor and the U.S. Department of Education and is designed especially for students like you. Here you'll find information on high-growth, high-demand occupations and the skills and education needed to attain those jobs.

Job Shadow *www.jobshadow.org*
See your future via a variety of on-line virtual job-shadowing videos and interviews featuring people with fascinating jobs.

My Cool Career *www.mycoolcareer.com*
This website touts itself as the "coolest career dream site for teens and 20's." See for yourself as you work your way through a variety of useful self-assessment quizzes, listen to an assortment of on-line career shows, and explore all kinds of career resources.

investigate local opportunities

To get a better understanding of employment happenings in your state, visit these state-specific career information websites.

Alabama
www.ajb.org/al
www.al.plusjobs.com

Alaska
www.jobs.state.ak.us
www.akcis.org/default.htm

Arizona
www.ajb.org/az
www.ade.state.az.us/cte/
  AZCrnproject10.asp

Arkansas
www.ajb.org/ar
www.careerwatch.org
www.ioscar.org/ar

California
www.calmis.ca.gov
www.ajb.org/ca
www.eurekanet.org

Colorado
www.coloradocareer.net
www.coworkforce.com/lmi

Connecticut
www1.ctdol.state.ct.us/jcc
www.ctdol.state.ct.us/lmi

Delaware
www.ajb.org/de
www.delewareworks.com

District of Columbia
www.ajb.org/dc
www.dcnetworks.org

Florida
www.Florida.access.bridges.com
www.employflorida.net

Georgia
www.gcic.peachnet.edu
  (Ask your school guidance coun
  selor for your school's free pass
  word and access code)
www.dol.state.ga.us/js

Hawaii
www.ajb.org/hi
www.careerkokua.org

Idaho
www.ajb.org/id
www.cis.idaho.gov

Illinois
www.ajb.org/il
www.ilworkinfo.com

Indiana
www.ajb.org/in
http://icpac.indiana.edu

Iowa
www.ajb.org/ia
www.state.ia.us/iccor

Kansas
www.ajb.org/ks
www.kansasjoblink.com/ada

Kentucky
www.ajb.org/ky

Louisiana
www.ajb.org/la
www.ldol.state.la.us/jobpage.asp

Maine
www.ajb.org/me
www.maine.gov/labor/lmis

Maryland
www.ajb.org/md
www.careernet.state.md.us

Massachusetts
www.ajb.org/ma
http://masscis.intocareers.org

Michigan
www.mois.org

Minnesota
www.ajb.org/mn
www.iseek.org

Mississippi
www.ajb.org/ms
www.mscareernet.org

Missouri
www.ajb.org/mo
www.greathires.org

Montana
www.ajb.org/mt
http://jsd.dli.state.mt.us/mjshome.asp

Nebraska
www.ajb.org/ne
www.careerlink.org

New Hampshire
www.nhes.state.nh.us

New Jersey
www.ajb.org/nj
www.wnjpin.net/coei

New Mexico
www.ajb.org/nm
www.dol.state.nm.us/soicc/upto21
  .html

Nevada
www.ajb.org/nv
http://nvcis.intocareers.org

New York
www.ajb.org/ny
www.nycareerzone.org

North Carolina
www.ajb.org/nc
www.ncsoicc.org
www.nccareers.org

North Dakota
www.ajb.org/nd
www.imaginend.com
www.ndcrn.com/students

Ohio
www.ajb.org/oh
https://scoti.ohio.gov/scoti_lexs

Oklahoma
www.ajb.org/ok
www.okcareertech.org/guidance
http://okcrn.org

Oregon
www.hsd.k12.or.us/crls

Pennsylvania
www.ajb.org/pa
www.pacareerlink.state.pa.us

Rhode Island
www.ajb.org/ri
www.dlt.ri.gov/lmi/jobseeker.htm

South Carolina
www.ajb.org/sc
www.scois.org/students.htm

South Dakota
www.ajb.org/sd

Tennessee
www.ajb.org/tn
www.tcids.utk.edu

Texas
www.ajb.org/tx
www.ioscar.org/tx
*www.cdr.state.tx.us/Hotline/Hotline
.html*

Utah
www.ajb.org/ut
http://jobs.utah.gov/wi/occi.asp

Vermont
www.ajb.org/vt
www.vermontjoblink.com
www.vtlmi.info/oic.cfm

Virginia
www.ajb.org/va
www.vacrn.net

Washington
www.ajb.org/wa
www.workforceexplorer.com
*www.wa.gov/esd/lmea/soicc/
sohome.htm*

West Virginia
www.ajb.org/wv
www.state.wv.us/bep/lmi

Wisconsin
www.ajb.org/wi
www.careers4wi.wisc.edu
*http://wiscareers.wisc.edu/splash.
asp*

Wyoming
www.ajb.org/wy
*http://uwadmnweb.uwyo.edu/SEO/
wcis.htm*

get a job

Whether you're curious about the kinds of jobs currently in big demand or you're actually looking for a job, the following websites are a great place to do some virtual job-hunting.

America's Job Bank *www.ajb.org*

Another example of your (or, more accurately, your parent's) tax dollars at work, this well-organized website is sponsored by the U.S. Department of Labor. Job seekers can post resumes and use the site's search engines to search through over a million job listings by location or by job type.

Monster.com *www.monster.com*

One of the Internet's most widely used employment websites, this is where you can search for specific types of jobs in specific parts of the country, network with millions of people, and find useful career advice.

explore by special interests

An especially effective way to explore career options is to look at careers associated with a personal interest or fascination with a certain type of industry. The following websites help you narrow down your options in a focused way.

What Interests You? *www.bls.gov/k12*

This Bureau of Labor Statistics website provides information about careers associated with 12 special interest areas: math, reading, science, social studies, music and arts, building and fixing things, helping people, computers, law, managing money, sports, and nature.

Construct My Future *www.constructmyfuture.com*

With over $600 billion annually devoted to new construction projects, about 6 million Americans build careers in this industry. This website, sponsored by the Association of Equipment Distributors, the Association of Equipment Manufacturers, and Associated General Contractors, introduces an interesting array of construction-related professions.

Dream It Do It *www.dreamit-doit.com*

In order to make manufacturing a preferred career choice by 2010, the National Association of Manufacturing's Center for Workforce Success is reaching out to young adults and their parents, educators, communities, and policy-makers to change their minds about manufacturing's future and its careers. This website introduces high-demand 21st-century manufacturing professions many will find surprising and worthy of serious consideration.

Get Tech *www.gettech.org*

Another award-winning website from the National Association of Manufacturing.

Take Another Look *www.Nrf.com/content/foundation/rcp/main.htm*

The National Retail Federation challenges students to take another look at their industry by introducing a wide variety of careers associated with marketing and advertising, store management, sales, distribution and logistics, e-commerce, and more.

Index

Page numbers in **boldface** indicate main articles. Page numbers in *italics* indicate photographs.

genetic testing 77
geneticist 30, 34, **76–78**
Genetics 76
Genetics Society of America 76
geriatric care 79, 80
geriatric nurse 140
geriatric optometrist 102
geriatric physical therapist 108
gerontologist 119
gerontology nurse 98
glaucoma 133
GlaxoSmithKline 95

histotechnologist 120
Hoffman–La Roche 45, 104
holistic medicine 37
Holland, John 17, 24
home health aide 30, 33, **79–80**
horticultural therapist 120
hospice care 79–80
hospital pharmacists 103
How CAT Scans Work (Web page) 57
How Stuff Works website 44, 46
Human Genome Project 48
hyperopia. *See* farsightedness

H

Handbook of Forensic Services 74
Harvard University 126
headaches 132
health care administrator 120
health care public relations 120
health educator 120
health informatics pathway 33
health information administrator 120
Health Promotion Career Network 84
health science
    work personality chart 29–30
health science librarian 120
health unit coordinator 120
Hearing Health Magazine 43
heart attack 100
Hebrew Academy of Cleveland 131
Hemapheresis ONline 105
herbal remedies 131, 133
Histo-Logic 59
histologic technician 120

I

immunologist 120
immunology (medical technologist) 89
Indiana 134
Indiana University School of Informatics 48
Industrial Hygiene, Informational Booklet on 81
industrial hygienist 30, **81–83**
infectious disease 134
informational interviews. *See* interviews, informational
insomnia 132
Institute for Genomic Research 76
interest assessment tool 3
interests and strengths 9–11, 116
International Federation for Medical and Biological Engineering 50
International Society for Environmental Epidemiology 72
internist 111, 120

skills, possessing right 116–118

skin puncture 105

slices (CT scans) 57

smallpox 138

social personality 22, 27

Social Security 93

social worker 120

Society of Nuclear Medicine 95, 96

sonographer 120

speech pathologist. *See* speech-language pathologist

speech-language pathologist 120. *See also* audiologist

    interview 131, 134, 136, 137, 139, 141

sports kinesiotherapist 84–85

sports massage 87

sports physical therapist 108

Sports Science Online 84

sports vision optometrist 102

Spotlight on Caregiving 79

Stamford, Connecticut 131

strengths and interests 9–11, 116

stroke 100

study cells 59

subluxation 53, 54

success lessons

    advice on 140–141

    career goal changes 134–135

    education 136

    finding the right career 132–134

    good choices and hard work 137–138

    influences on you 138–139

    job pros and cons 135–136

    learning from others' mistakes 140

support services pathway 34

surgeon 111, 120

surgery nurse 98

surgical assistant 120

surgical technologist 120

Susan G. Komen Breast Cancer Foundation 59

Swedish massage 87

T

Tampa Bay Devil Rays 131

teachers 43

Tempe, Arizona 131

terrorism, chemical and biological 72

Thai massage 87

therapeutic recreation specialist 120

therapeutic services pathway 33

Third Watch 69

thoracic surgeon 120

3M 90

Toronto, Canada 139

toxicologists 74

tracers. *See* radioactive materials

training requirements 149, 151

U

UCLA Medical School 139

urologist 120

U.S. Army's Dental Care System 63

Virtual Library of Epidemiology 72
vision researcher 102
visual therapy 133
vocational-rehabilitation counselor
  120

W

Walter Reed Army Hospital 131
Whitaker Foundation 50
WIP. *See* Work Interest Profiler
Work Interest Profiler (WIP)
  health science careers work
    personality chart 29–30
  completing 18
  described 18
  evaluating 24
  sections 19–23
work personality
  finding 3–4, 17–18
  matching with careers 116
  types of
    artistic personality 22, 26
    conventional personality 23,
      28
    enterprising personality 23,
      27

investigative personality 21,
  25
realistic personality 21, 25
social personality 22, 27
Work Interest Profiler (WIP)
  18–30
work personality chart
  health science careers 29–30
work personality codes 29–30
work values 12–16, 116
workplace kinesiotherapist 85
workplaces, types of 148–149,
  151

X

X rays 57

Y

yoga 53
York University 139
*Young Forensic Scientists Forum
  Newsletter* 74